Strategic Intervention
Teacher Activity Guide

Houghton
Mifflin
Harcourt

RtI Response to Intervention
Tier 2 Activities

Grade 1

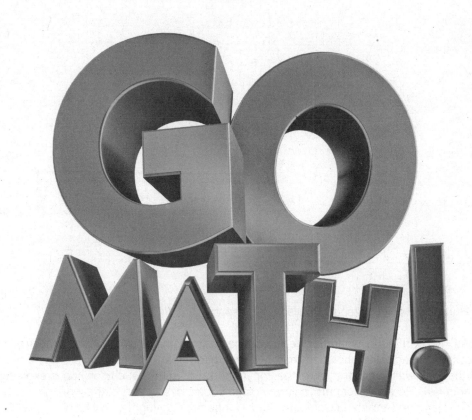

INCLUDES:
- Diagnostic Practice for Prerequisite Skills
- Activities for Students Needing Tier 2 Instructional Intervention
- Copying Masters

ISBN 978-0-544-24903-5

6 7 8 9 10 1409 22 21 20 19 18 17 16 15

4500530482   A B C D E F G

Contents

SKILLS

PROBLEM SOLVING STRATEGIES

Tier 2 and Tier 3 Intervention Resources

Using the Tier 2 and Tier 3 print and online Intervention Resources help children build a solid foundation of mathematical ideas and concepts. *Go Math! Response to Intervention • Tier 2 Activities* are designed for children who need small group instruction to review prerequisite concepts and skills needed for the chapter. *Go Math! Response to Intervention • Tier 3 Activities* are targeted at children who need one-on-one instruction to build foundational skills for the chapter. By focusing on essential prerequisite skills and concepts for each chapter, the tiered intervention skills prescribe instruction to prepare children to work successfully on grade-level content. The *Go Math! Response to Intervention • Tier 2 Activities, Response to Intervention • Tier 3 Activities*, and *Personal Math Trainer Math* resources help you accommodate the diverse skill levels of your children at all levels of intervention.

How do I determine if a child needs intervention?

Before beginning each chapter, have children complete the *Show What You Know* page in the *Go Math! Student Edition*. *Show What You Know* targets the prerequisite skills necessary for success in each chapter and allows you to diagnose a child's need for intervention. Alternatively, at the beginning of the school year, the Prerequisite Skills Test in the *Assessment Guide* can be used.

In what format are the intervention materials?

A. *Go Math! Response to Intervention • Tier 2 Activities* include the *Strategic Intervention Teacher Activity Guide*, which includes copying masters for skill development and skill practice and teacher support pages. The copying masters can be used by individual children or small groups. The teacher support pages provide teaching suggestions for skill development, as well as an Alternative Teaching Strategy for children who continue to have difficulty with a skill.

B. *Go Math! Response to Intervention • Tier 3 Activities* include the *Intensive Intervention Teacher Guide* and *Intensive Intervention Skill Packs* for Grades K–6. A separate *User Guide/Activity Guide* correlates *Intensive Intervention* Tier 3 skills and an Alternative Teaching Activity to each chapter of the *Go Math!* program.

C. *Personal Math Trainer* provides online skill development, and practice for all levels of intervention in an electronic format. *Personal Math Trainer* features pre-built assignments for intervention and practice. Children receive feedback on incorrect answers and learning aids help them develop clear insight into underlying concepts as they build toward an understanding of on-level skills.

Using Response to Intervention • Tier 2 Activities

What materials and resources do I need for intervention?

The teaching strategies may require the use of common classroom manipulatives or easily gathered classroom objects. Since these activities are designed only for those children who show weaknesses in their skill development, the quantity of materials will be small. For many activities, you may substitute materials, such as paper squares for tiles, coins for two-color counters, and so on.

How are the skill lessons in *Response to Intervention • Tier 2 Activities* structured?

Each skill lesson in the Teacher Activity Guide includes two student pages, a page of teacher support, and an answer key for the student pages.

The student lesson begins with *Learn the Math* — a guided page that provides a model or an explanation of the skill.

The second part of the lesson is *Do the Math* — a selection of exercises that provide practice and may be completed independently, with a partner, or with teacher direction. This page provides scaffolded exercises, which gradually remove prompts.

Children who have difficulty with the *Do the Math* exercises may benefit from the Alternative Teaching Strategy activity provided on the teacher support page of each lesson.

How can I organize my classroom and schedule time for intervention?

You may want to set up a Math Skill Center with a record folder for each child. Based on a child's performance on the *Show What You Know* page, assign prescribed skills by marking the child's record folder. The child can then work through the intervention materials, record the date of completion, and place the completed work in a folder for your review. Children might visit the Math Skill Center for a specified time during the day, two or three times a week, or during free time. You may wish to assign children a partner, assign a small group to work together, or work with individuals one-on-one.

Grade 1
Strategic Intervention: Response to Intervention • Tier 2
Chapter Correlations

Skill Number	Skill Title	*SWYK Chapter
1	Numbers 1–10	Addition Concepts; Subtraction Concepts
2	Zero	Addition Concepts
3	Use Pictures to Subtract	Subtraction Concepts
4	Use Symbols to Add	Addition Strategies
5	Add in Any Order	Addition Strategies
6	Use Symbols to Subtract	Subtraction Strategies
7	Subtract All or Zero	Subtraction Strategies
8	Count On	Addition and Subtraction Relationships
9	Count Back	Addition and Subtraction Relationships
10	Count Groups to 20	Count and Model Numbers; Two-Digit Addition and Subtraction
11	Make Groups of 10	Count and Model Numbers
12	More, Fewer	Compare Numbers; Represent Data
13	Draw Equal Groups	Compare Numbers; Represent Data
15	Use a Hundred Chart to Count	Two-Digit Addition and Subtraction
18	Identify Three-Dimensional Shapes	Three-Dimensional Geometry
19	Identify Two-Dimensional Shapes	Two-Dimensional Geometry
22	Compare Length	Measurement
26	Sort by Size	Three-Dimensional Geometry
27	Sort Shapes	Two-Dimensional Geometry

*SWYK refers to the *Show What You Know* page at the beginning of each chapter.

Objective
To count, read, and write to identify numbers to 10

Manipulatives and Materials
counters, ten frames (see *Teacher Resources*)

COMMON ERROR

- Children may not understand that numbers can be shown in different ways.

- To help them identify numbers that are shown in different ways, encourage children to write numbers and to use counters and pictures to represent numbers.

Learn the Math page IN3 Read and discuss some ways to show numbers with children. Guide them through the exercises at the bottom of the page. In Exercise 1, elicit from children that the number word *seven* is not the same as the other numbers. In Exercise 2, point out that the number of pencils is not the same as the other numbers. Ask: **How many pencils are there?** 9 pencils

REASONING Draw 5 counters (in a ten frame) on the board. Below the counters, draw 3 stick figures (or some other simple picture). Ask: **Do the pictures show the same number as the counters? Explain.** No; possible answer: there are 5 counters, but there are only 3 stick figures. Count the counters and figures drawn on the board with the children. Explain that the numbers are not the same.

Do the Math page IN4 Read and discuss Exercise 1 with children. Have them model 7 counters on a ten frame. Ask: **How many counters are there?** 7 counters Guide children to draw a picture to show the number.

Assign Exercises 2–5 and monitor children's work.

Guide children to read the first sentence in Problem 6. Invite children to point out the number word *ten* in the sentence and then write the number 10.

Children who make more than 1 error in Exercises 1–6 may benefit from the **Alternative Teaching Strategy**.

Alternative Teaching Strategy
Materials: numeral cards and dot cards for 1–10 (see *Teacher Resources*)

Make a memory game using numeral cards and dot cards for 1–10. Cut out each card and place cards facedown in a grid pattern. Have a player turn over two cards. If the numbers on both cards are the same, the player can take another turn. If not, the cards are turned back again for the next player.

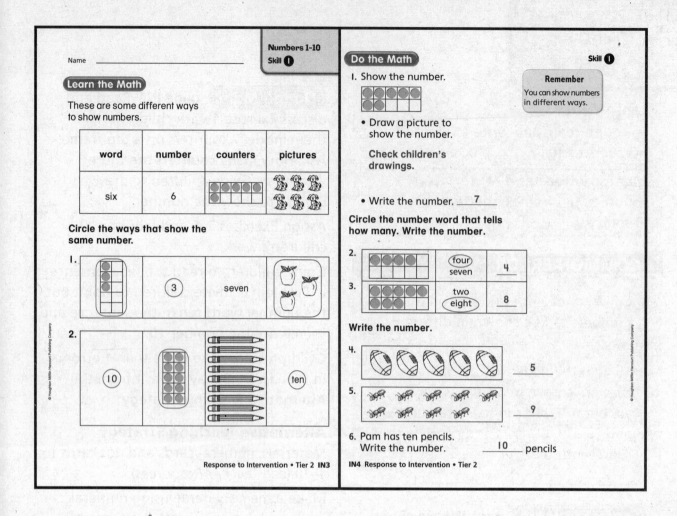

Learn the Math

These are some different ways
to show numbers.

word	number	counters	pictures
six	6		

**Circle the ways that show the
same number.**

1.

3   seven

2.

10   ten

Do the Math

1. Show the number.

- Draw a picture to
  show the number.

  Check children's
  drawings.

- Write the number. ___7___

**Circle the number word that tells
how many. Write the number.**

2.

four
seven   4

3.

two
eight   8

Write the number.

4.

5

5.

9

6. Pam has ten pencils.
   Write the number. ___10___ pencils

Name _____

Learn the Math

These are some different ways
to show numbers.

word	number	counters	pictures
six	6	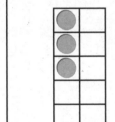	

**Circle the ways that show the
same number.**

1.

3

seven

2.

1 0

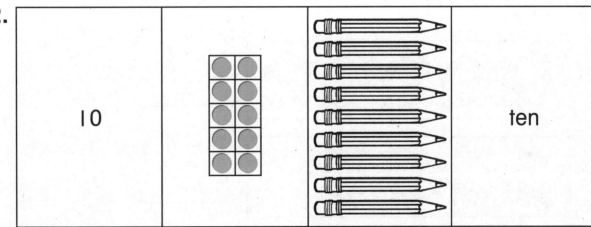

ten

Do the Math

1. Show the number.

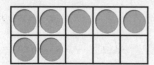

Remember
You can show numbers in different ways.

- Draw a picture to show the number.

- Write the number. _____

Circle the number word that tells how many. Write the number.

2.	four seven	_____
3.	two eight	_____

Write the number.

4.

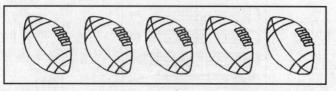

_____

5.

_____

6. Pam has ten pencils.
Write the number. _____ pencils

Objective

To recognize and write the numeral that describes the quantity zero

Vocabulary

zero A cardinal number indicating an empty set

COMMON ERROR

- Children may not understand when to use 0.

- To correct this, have children count backward while removing one item at a time from a group. This will help children visualize that when there are no items left in the group they have reached the number 0.

Learn the Math page IN7 Read the direction line with children. On the board, model how to write a zero. Monitor children as they practice writing zero. Work through the examples with the children. Point out that when there are no birds to count, there are zero birds. In the last example, have children count the number of apples in the tree. Since there are no apples, have children write the number 0. For further reinforcement, instruct children to color the tree that has zero birds or zero apples.

REASONING Ask: **How can you tell that the first picture shows zero birds?** There are no birds to count in the picture. Point out that when the number 2 is shown using pictures, there will be 2 objects to count. When the number zero is shown, there will not be any objects to count.

Do the Math page IN8 Ask: **What does the number zero mean?** The number zero means there are none. Read and discuss Exercise 1. Point out the bulleted question. Ask: **Are there any counters in the box? Explain.** No; possible answer: I looked in the box. There are no counters in the box. Guide children to count the counters in the box and to write the number 0.

Assign Exercises 2–7 and monitor children's work.

Guide children to read the sentence in Problem 8. Remind children that the glass that has 0 ice cubes is the glass with no ice cubes in it. For Problem 9, explain to children that the basket that has 0 apples is the basket with no apples in it.

Children who make more than 2 errors in Exercises 1–9 may benefit from the **Alternative Teaching Strategy**.

Alternative Teaching Strategy

Ask children counting questions about classroom objects. For example, "How many clocks are in the classroom?" or "How many zebras are in the classroom?" Include plenty of *zero* responses. Be sure to limit the number of objects in a set to ten. Invite volunteers to count the objects and tell the number. Write the number 0 on the board with each response of zero.

Name _____

Learn the Math

Zero means none. Practice writing zero.

0 O O · · · · · ·
zero

Vocabulary
zero

Write how many.

There are no birds.
The number of birds is 0.

0

There are six birds.
The number of birds is 6.

6

There are no apples.
The number of apples is 0.

0

Response to Intervention • Tier 2 **IN7**

Do the Math

I. How many ● are in the box?

- Are there any ●? no
- Count the ●.
- Write how many ●. 0

Remember
Zero means none.

Count the objects.
Write how many.

2. 2

3. 0

4. 0

5. 5

6. 4

7. 0

8. Circle the glass that
has 0 ice cubes.

9. Circle the basket that
has 0 apples.

Name _____

Learn the Math

Zero means none. Practice writing zero.

0 0̸ 0̸ · · · · ·

zero

Vocabulary

zero

Write how many.

There are no birds.

The number of birds is 0.

0̸
___

There are six birds.

The number of birds is 6.

6̸
___

There are no apples.

The number of apples is 0.

0̸
___

1. How many 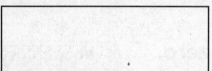 are in the box?

  · Are there any 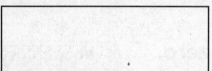? _____

  · Count the 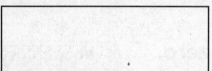.

  · Write how many 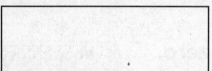. _____

Count the objects.
Write how many.

2.  _____

3. _____

4. _____

5.  _____

6.  _____

7. _____

8. Circle the glass that has 0 ice cubes.

9. Circle the basket that has 0 apples.

Use Pictures to Subtract
Skill 3

Objective
To use pictures to subtract

Manipulatives
counters

COMMON ERROR

- Children may not visualize the part that is being taken away in subtraction problems.

- To correct this, have children act out the problems with counters. Children can show the number they start with, and then physically take away the group they are subtracting.

Learn the Math page IN11 Have children look at the picture as you read the story aloud. Tell children that they can use the picture to solve the problem. Say: **There are three bees in the garden.** Have children point to each bee. Say: **Then two bees fly away.** Discuss ways children might show two bees flying away. Have children circle the group of two bees and mark an X over the group. Once children have crossed out 2 bees, ask: **How many bees are left?** 1 bee

REASONING Encourage children to use counters to represent the bees in the math story. Ask: **How could you show the math story using counters?** Possible answer: I could show 3 counters, and then take 2 away.

Do the Math page IN12 Read and discuss Exercise 1 with children. Guide them through the bulleted questions as they count the number of pears, the number subtracted, and the number left. Explain to children that the circle and X over the group indicates that it is being subtracted. You may wish to make up a math story to go with the subtraction problem to help children understand the concept.

Assign Exercises 2–7 and monitor children's work.

Read Problem 8 with children. Invite volunteers to answer questions about the math story. Ask: **How many apples does Lela have?** 4 apples **How many apples does she eat?** 2 apples Encourage children to circle the group of two apples Lela eats and then mark an X on that group. Have children write the number of apples left, 2 apples.

Children who make more than 2 errors in Exercises 1–8 may benefit from the **Alternative Teaching Strategy**.

Alternative Teaching Strategy
Materials: paper, crayons

Have children draw several of the same kind of object on a sheet of paper. Then have children use the drawing to construct a subtraction story problem. For example, one child may draw 5 bouncing balls. Then the child may circle and mark an X over 3 of the 5 balls. Encourage children to share the subtraction story problem with the class. Invite volunteers to tell how many objects are in the picture, how many objects are being subtracted, and how many objects are left.

Name _____

Learn the Math

There are 3 bees in the garden.
Then 2 bees fly away.
How many bees are left?

You can use a picture to subtract.

- How many bees are in the garden?
  __3__ bees

- How many bees fly away?
  __2__ bees

- Circle the group that flies away.
  Mark an X on that group.

- How many bees are left?
  __l__ bee

So, $3 - 2 =$ __l__.

Response to Intervention • Tier 2 **IN11**

Use the picture to subtract.

1.
   $4 - 1 =$ __3__

- How many pears
  do you see? __4__ pears

- How many will you subtract? __l__ pear

- How many are left? __3__ pears

So, $4 - 1 =$ __3__.

Remember
Use the picture
to subtract.

Use the picture. Write how many are left.

2.  $3 - 1 =$ __2__	3. $5 - 4 =$ __l__
4. $5 - 2 =$ __3__	5. $4 - 3 =$ __l__
6. $3 - 2 =$ __l__	7. $6 - 4 =$ __2__

Mark the picture to show subtraction. Solve.

8. Lela has 4 apples. She eats
   2 apples. How many apples
   does she have left?

   __2__ apples

IN12 Response to Intervention • Tier 2

Learn the Math

There are 3 bees in the garden.
Then 2 bees fly away.
How many bees are left?

You can use a picture to subtract.

- How many bees are in the garden?

  _____ bees

- How many bees fly away?

  _____ bees

- Circle the group that flies away.
  Mark an X on that group.

- How many bees are left?

  _____ bee

So, $3 - 2 =$ _____.

Use the picture to subtract.

1.

   $4 - 1 =$ _____

   · How many pears
     do you see? _____ pears

   · How many will you subtract? _____ pear

   · How many are left? _____ pears

   So, $4 - 1 =$ _____.

Use the picture. Write how many are left.

2.

   $3 - 1 =$ _____

3.

   $5 - 4 =$ _____

4.

   $5 - 2 =$ _____

5.

   $4 - 3 =$ _____

6.

   $3 - 2 =$ _____

7.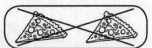

   $6 - 4 =$ _____

Mark the picture to show subtraction. Solve.

8. Lela has 4 apples. She eats
   2 apples. How many apples
   does she have left?

   _____ apples

Use Symbols to Add
Skill 4

Objective
To use pictures and symbols to write addition sentences

Vocabulary
plus (+)

is equal to (=)

sum The answer to an addition problem

addition sentence 3 + 4 = 7

Manipulatives
counters

COMMON ERROR

- Children may not use the symbols in the correct order.

- To correct this, have children read the number sentences aloud to see if they make sense.

Learn the Math page IN15 Read through the problem with children and discuss the three steps: See, Say, and Write. Point out and name the + and = symbols in the addition sentence. Ask: **What is a sum?** A sum is the answer to an addition problem. Ask: **So, how many goldfish does Jameel have in all?** 5 goldfish

Work through Exercises 1–2 with children. If you wish, have children use counters to represent the pictures.

REASONING Ask: **What are the symbols for *plus* and *is equal to*?** + and = Have a volunteer write the symbols on the board. Have another volunteer use the symbols to write an addition sentence.

Do the Math page IN16 Read and discuss Exercise 1 with children. Ask: **Which two symbols can you use in this sentence?** + and = **What do these two symbols stand for?** *plus* and *is equal to* Complete Exercise 1 with children. Guide them to write the addition sentence.

Assign Exercises 2–5 and monitor children's work.

As children read Problem 6, encourage them to draw pictures or use counters to represent the baseball cards. Have children make one group of 5 baseball cards and one group of 4 baseball cards. Then have children write the numbers and symbols in an addition sentence to show the total number of baseball cards Steve has.

Children who make more than 1 error in Exercises 1–6 may benefit from the **Alternative Teaching Strategy**.

Alternative Teaching Strategy
Manipulatives and Materials: counters, paper bags, index cards

Place ten counters in a paper bag for each pair of children. Give each pair an index card. Have each child pull a few counters from the bag. On the same index card, guide one partner to draw the number of counters he or she pulled from the bag and have the other partner do the same. Then have partners use the correct symbols to write the addition sentence on the index card to show how many counters the pair pulled all together.

Learn the Math

You can write an addition sentence with + and =.

Vocabulary
plus (+)
is equal to (=)
sum
addition sentence

Jameel has 2 goldfish. Then he gets 3 more. How many goldfish does he have in all?

Step 1 See.	🐟🐟 🐟🐟🐟
Step 2 Say.	2 plus 3 is equal to 5. The sum is 5.
Step 3 Write.	2 (+) 3 (=) 5

So, Jameel has __5__ goldfish in all.

Use the picture. Write the addition sentence.

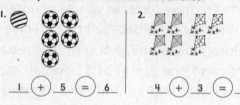

1. __1__ (+) __5__ (=) __6__

2. __4__ (+) __3__ (=) __7__

Do the Math

Skill ④

**Use the picture.
Write the addition sentence.**

Remember
plus (+)
is equal to (=)

The answer in an addition sentence is called the sum.

1. 💡💡💡💡 💡💡💡

- What is the first number? __4__
- What number are you adding? __3__
- What is the sum? __7__

__4__ (+) __3__ (=) __7__

2.

__3__ (+) __5__ (=) __8__

3.

__5__ (+) __3__ (=) __8__

4.

__4__ (+) __2__ (=) __6__

5. 🪑🪑🪑 🪑🪑 🪑🪑

__7__ (+) __2__ (=) __9__

**Draw a picture to solve.
Write the addition sentence.**

6. Steve has 5 baseball cards. He buys 4 more cards. How many cards does Steve have now?

Check children's drawings.

__5__ (+) __4__ (=) __9__

__9__ cards

Name _____

Learn the Math

You can write an addition sentence
with + and =.

Jameel has 2 goldfish. Then he
gets 3 more. How many goldfish
does he have in all?

Step 1 See.	🐟 🐟 🐟 🐟 🐟
Step 2 Say.	2 plus 3 is equal to 5. The sum is 5.
Step 3 Write.	2 ⊕ 3 ⊜ 5

So, Jameel has _____ goldfish in all.

Use the picture. Write the addition sentence.

1.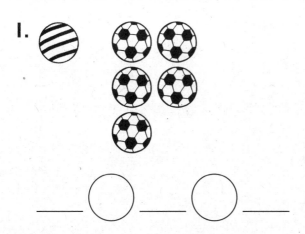

   ___ ◯ ___ ◯ ___

2.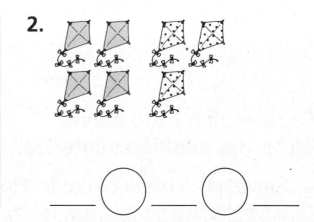

   ___ ◯ ___ ◯ ___

Use the picture.
Write the addition sentence.

1.

- What is the first number? _____
- What number are you adding? _____
- What is the sum? _____

___ ◯ ___ ___ ◯ ___

2.

___ ◯ ___ ___ ◯ ___

3.

___ ◯ ___ ___ ◯ ___

4.

___ ◯ ___ ___ ◯ ___

5.

___ ◯ ___ ___ ◯ ___

Draw a picture to solve.
Write the addition sentence.

6. Steve has 5 baseball cards. He buys 4 more cards. How many cards does Steve have now?

___ ◯ ___ ◯ ___

_____ cards

Add in Any Order
Skill 5

Objective
To add using the Commutative Property

Vocabulary
order A particular arrangement of things one after the other

addend Any of the numbers that are added

Manipulatives
two-color counters

COMMON ERROR

- Children may not understand that the order of the addends can be changed in an addition sentence.

- To correct this, demonstrate that the sum stays the same even if the order of the addends is changed.

Learn the Math page IN19 Have children look at the first row of cars. Ask: **How many gray cars are there?** 3 gray cars **How many white cars are there?** 2 white cars **How many cars are there in all?** 5 cars Repeat the activity with the second row of cars. Then ask: **How is the second row of cars different from the first row of cars?** Possible answer: the first row of cars shows 3 and 2. The second row of cars shows 2 and 3. Elicit from children that the addends in both addition sentences are the same, but the order of the addends is different. In both addition sentences, the sum is the same. Encourage children to use counters to model Exercise 1.

REASONING Ask: How is $5 + 1 = 6$ the same as $1 + 5 = 6$? How is it different? Possible answer: the two addition sentences have the same addends and sum, but the addends are in a different order in each sentence.

Do the Math page IN20 Read and discuss Exercise 1 with children. Encourage them to use counters to model the problem. Ask: **Will the sum change when you change the order of the addends?** no Guide them through the steps. Ask: **Is the sum the same in both addition sentences?** yes

Assign Exercises 2–4 and monitor children's work.

Guide children to read Problem 5. Help them find the addends in the problem. Children may wish to use counters or draw a picture to find the sum. Then have them write the addition sentence. For the second addition sentence, have them change the order of the addends.

Children who make more than 1 error in Exercises 1–5 may benefit from the **Alternative Teaching Strategy**.

Alternative Teaching Strategy
Have a few children act out addition problems. Have a small group of children represent one addend. Have another group of children represent the other addend. Have the class find the sum of the two groups of children. Then have the two groups trade locations. Have the class find the sum. Guide children to see that the order of the addends in an addition sentence can be changed and the sum stays the same.

Name _____

Learn the Math

You can change the order of the addends. The sum is the same.

$3 + 2 = \underline{5}$

↑   ↑   ↑

addends   sum

There are $\underline{5}$ cars in all.

Change the order of the addends.
Write the addition sentence.

$2 (+) 3 (\div) 5$

↑   ↑   ↑

addends   sum

There are $\underline{5}$ cars in all.

Write the sum. Change the order of the addends. Write the addition sentence.

1.

$4 + 2 = \underline{6}$ $2 (+) 4 (=) 6$

Do the Math

1.

- What are the addends? $\underline{2}$ and $\underline{6}$
- So, $2 + 6 = \underline{8}$.
- Change the order of the addends.
  Write the addition sentence.

$6 (+) 2 (=) 8$

Write the sum. Change the order of the addends. Write the addition sentence.

2.

$5 + 3 = \underline{8}$ $3 (+) 5 (=) 8$

3. $4 + 6 = \underline{10}$ $6 (+) 4 (=) 10$

4. $7 + 2 = \underline{9}$ $2 (+) 7 (=) 9$

Write two addition sentences to solve.

5. Kip has 2 gray cars. He has 5 white cars. How many cars does Kip have in all?

$2 (+) 5 (=) 7$

$5 (+) 2 (=) 7$

$\underline{7}$ cars

Learn the Math

You can change the order of the addends.
The sum is the same.

Vocabulary

order

addend

3 + 2 = _5_

↑   ↑   ↑

  addends   sum

There are _5_ cars in all.

Change the order of the addends.
Write the addition sentence.

_2_ (+) _3_ (=) _5_

↑   ↑   ↑

  addends   sum

There are _5_ cars in all.

**Write the sum. Change the order of the
addends. Write the addition sentence.**

1.  |

  4 + 2 = ___ | ___ ◯ ___ ◯ ___

1.

- What are the addends? ____ and ____

- So, $2 + 6 =$ ____.

- Change the order of the addends.
  Write the addition sentence.

  ___ ◯ ___ ◯ ___

Write the sum. Change the order of the addends. Write the addition sentence.

2.

$5 + 3 =$ ____   ___ ◯ ___ ◯ ___

3. $4 + 6 =$ ____   ___ ◯ ___ ◯ ___

4. $7 + 2 =$ ____   ___ ◯ ___ ◯ ___

Write two addition sentences to solve.

5. Kip has 2 gray cars. He has 5 white cars. How many cars does Kip have in all?

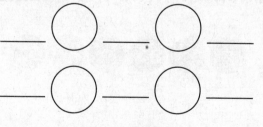

____ cars

Use Symbols to Subtract
Skill 6

Objective
To use pictures and symbols to write subtraction sentences

Vocabulary
minus (−)
is equal to (=)
difference The answer to a subtraction problem
subtraction sentence $9 − 6 = 3$

Manipulatives
counters

COMMON ERROR

- Children may think that the order of the first two numbers in a subtraction sentence does not matter.

- To correct this, explain that they should start with the greater number, or the whole group, and then take the lesser number away.

Learn the Math page IN23 Read the problem with the children. Discuss the three steps: See, Say, and Write. Point out and name the − and = symbols in the subtraction sentence. Ask: **What is a difference?** A difference is the answer to a subtraction problem.

Work through Exercises 1–4 with children. Remind them to use the pictures, or counters to represent the pictures, to solve the problem. Guide them to write the number showing the whole group, followed by a subtraction symbol, followed by the number shown by the group that is crossed out. The difference is shown by the pictures that are not crossed out.

REASONING Ask: **What are the symbols for *minus* and *is equal to*?** -- and = Invite volunteers to give an example of the correct use of the symbols. Discuss how the symbols look and what they stand for.

Do the Math page IN24 Read and discuss Exercise 1 with children. Ask: **Which two symbols are used in this sentence?** − and = **What do these two symbols stand for?** *minus* and *is equal to* Guide children to write the subtraction sentence.

Assign Exercises 2–4 and monitor children's work.

After children read Problem 5, encourage them to use the pictures. Have children find how many are being subtracted. Then have them write the numbers and symbols in a subtraction sentence.

Children who make more than 1 error in Exercises 1–5 may benefit from the **Alternative Teaching Strategy**.

Alternative Teaching Strategy
Materials: paper, crayons

Have children draw several of the same kind of simple picture on a sheet of paper. For example, one child might draw 8 cars. Then have partners exchange papers. Have them circle a group to take away and then cross it out. For example, one child might take away a group of 3 cars. Have partners exchange papers again and then use the correct symbols to write a subtraction sentence that corresponds to the picture.

Name _____

Learn the Math

You can write a subtraction sentence with − and =.

Sam has 5 apples. He gives 2 apples to Mary. Sam has 3 apples left.

minus (−)
is equal to (=)
difference
subtraction sentence

Step 1 See.	🍎🍎🍎🍎
Step 2 Say.	5 minus 2 is equal to 3. The difference is 3.
Step 3 Write.	5 ⊖ 2 ⊜ 3

Use the picture. Write the subtraction sentence.

1. 5 (−) 3 (=) 2

2. 7 (−) 2 (=) 5

3. 4 (−) 1 (=) 3

4. 8 (−) 4 (=) 4

Response to Intervention • Tier 2 **IN23**

**Use the picture.
Write the subtraction sentence.**

1.
- How many are there in all? __6__
- How many do you subtract? __2__
- What is the difference? __4__

  6 (−) 2 (=) 4

2. 6 (−) 5 (=) 1

3. 5 (−) 1 (=) 4

4. 8 (−) 5 (=) 3

5. Brad has 6 ice cubes. 2 ice cubes melt. How many ice cubes does Brad have left?

   6 (−) 2 (=) 4

IN24 Response to Intervention • Tier 2

Name _____

Learn the Math

You can write a subtraction sentence with − and =.

Sam has 5 apples. He gives 2 apples to Mary. Sam has 3 apples left.

Step 1 See.	![apples](three apples and one circled pair crossed out)
Step 2 Say.	5 minus 2 is equal to 3. The difference is 3.
Step 3 Write.	5 ⊖ 2 ⊜ 3

Use the picture. Write the subtraction sentence.

1.  ___ ◯ ___ ◯ ___

2.  ___ ◯ ___ ◯ ___

3. 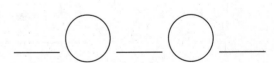 ___ ◯ ___ ◯ ___

4.  ___ ◯ ___ ◯ ___

Use the picture.
Write the subtraction sentence.

1.

   · How many are there in all? _____

   · How many do you subtract? _____

   · What is the difference? _____

   ____ ◯ ____ ◯ ____

2.    ____ ◯ ____ ◯ ____

3.    ____ ◯ ____ ◯ ____

4. 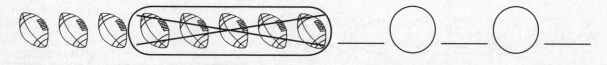   ____ ◯ ____ ◯ ____

5. Brad has 6 ice cubes. 2 ice cubes melt. How many ice cubes does Brad have left?

   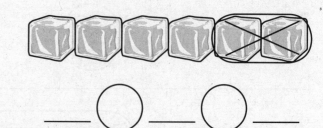

   ____ ◯ ____ ◯ ____

Name _____

Learn the Math

You can subtract zero or all from a number.

Subtract 0. The same number is left.	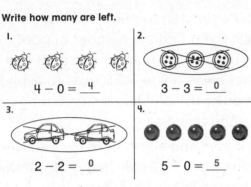 $3 - 0 = \underline{3}$
Subtract all. 0 are left.	$5 - 5 = \underline{0}$

Write how many are left.

1.

$4 - 0 = \underline{4}$

2.

$3 - 3 = \underline{0}$

3.

$2 - 2 = \underline{0}$

4.

$5 - 0 = \underline{5}$

Write how many are left.

1.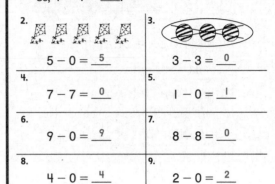

- How many soccer balls are there? $\underline{4}$
- How many are taken away? $\underline{4}$
- How many are left? $\underline{0}$

So, $4 - 4 = \underline{0}$.

Remember
- Subtract 0 and the same number is left.
- Subtract all and 0 are left.

2.

$5 - 0 = \underline{5}$

3.

$3 - 3 = \underline{0}$

4. $7 - 7 = \underline{0}$

5. $1 - 0 = \underline{1}$

6. $9 - 0 = \underline{9}$

7. $8 - 8 = \underline{0}$

8. $4 - 0 = \underline{4}$

9. $2 - 0 = \underline{2}$

10. Liz has 6 books. She gives all of the books to Sam. How many books does Liz have left?

$\underline{0}$ books

Objective
To subtract all or zero from a number

COMMON ERROR

- Children may confuse subtracting zero and subtracting all.

- To correct this, have children count back while removing one object from a group as each number is said.

Learn the Math page IN27 Have children look at the picture of apples as you read about subtracting 0. Ask: **How many apples are taken away?** 0 apples **How many apples are left?** 3 apples Have children look at the picture of acorns as you read about subtracting all. Ask: **How many acorns are taken away?** 5 acorns **How many acorns are left?** 0 acorns

REASONING Have children look at the picture of apples. Say: **Suppose you have 6 apples.** Ask: **When you subtract 0 apples from 6 apples, how many apples are left? Explain.** Possible answer: six apples are left because that is the number you started with.

Do the Math page IN28 Guide children to solve Exercise 1. Remind them that the X and circle over the group indicate that part is taken away from the whole group. You might want to tell a math story that corresponds to the subtraction problem.

Assign Exercises 2–9 and monitor children's work.

Guide children to read Problem 10. Help them find the number of books Liz has and the number of books she gives away. Invite volunteers to explain whether the problem is subtracting zero or subtracting all.

Children who make more than 2 errors in Exercises 1–10 may benefit from the **Alternative Teaching Strategy**.

Alternative Teaching Strategy
Have children stand up or sit down when a subtract all or a subtract zero problem is read. If the answer is 0, children sit down. If the answer is the same number as the number subtracted from, they stand up. For example, say: $5 - 0$. Since the answer is the same number, the children should stand. Then say: $5 - 5$. Since the answer is 0, they should sit down.

Name _____

Learn the Math

You can subtract zero or all from a number.

Subtract 0. The same number is left.	 $3 - 0 = \underline{3}$
Subtract all. 0 are left.	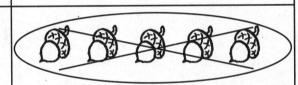 $5 - 5 = \underline{0}$

Write how many are left.

1.

$4 - 0 = \underline{}$

2.

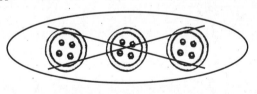

$3 - 3 = \underline{}$

3.

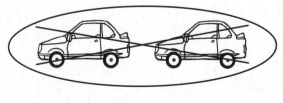

$2 - 2 = \underline{}$

4.

$5 - 0 = \underline{}$

Write how many are left.

1.

- How many soccer balls are there? ____

- How many are taken away? ____

- How many are left? ____

So, 4 − 4 = ____.

2.

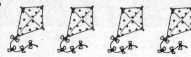

5 − 0 = ____

3.

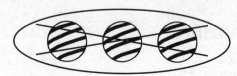

3 − 3 = ____

4.

7 − 7 = ____

5.

1 − 0 = ____

6.

9 − 0 = ____

7.

8 − 8 = ____

8.

4 − 0 = ____

9.

2 − 0 = ____

10. Liz has 6 books. She gives all of the books to Sam. How many books does Liz have left?

____ books

Objective

To use a number line to count on to add

Vocabulary

number line A line marked with a sequence of numbers at regularly spaced points along its length

count on To count forward from a given number

COMMON ERROR

- Children may count back instead of counting on.

- To correct this, remind children to count to the right on the number line.

Learn the Math page IN31 Discuss the number line with children. Point out that to count on, or add, they must move to the right. If children have difficulty remembering which is right, point out that the numbers become greater as they move in that direction.

Model the example with children. Ask: **What number are you starting with?** 7 Demonstrate for children where to start on the number line and how to make jumps to the right to count on. Model Exercises 1–8 with children.

REASONING Say: **Kalil says that 10 + 2 = 13.** Ask: **Do you agree?** No; Possible answer: If I start on 10 and count on 2, the sum is 12. Monitor how children use the number line to solve the problem.

Do the Math page IN32 Work through Exercise 1 with children. Guide children to see how the problem is really an addition problem that can be solved by counting on.

Assign Exercises 2–11 and monitor children's work.

Read Problem 12 with children. Encourage them to use a number line. Have them start with the greater number and count on to find the sum.

Children who make more than 3 errors in Exercises 1–12 may benefit from the **Alternative Teaching Strategy**.

Alternative Teaching Strategy

Materials: adhesive tape

Have children use a floor number line to count on. Construct a number line on the floor with adhesive tape or other material. Write some addition sentences on the board that involve adding 1, 2, or 3. Invite volunteers to take turns using the number line to count on. Have children start with the greater number and then make jumps to count on.

Name _____

Learn the Math

Use a number line to count on.

- What is $7 + 3$?
- Start on the greater number.
- Make jumps to the right.
- Write the sum.

Vocabulary
number line
count on

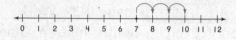

So, $7 + 3 = \underline{10}$.

Use the number line to add. Write each sum.

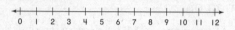

1. $4 + 3 = \underline{7}$

2. $8 + 2 = \underline{10}$

3. $5 + 1 = \underline{6}$

4. $3 + 9 = \underline{12}$

5. $6 + 1 = \underline{7}$

6. $2 + 7 = \underline{9}$

7. $3 + 5 = \underline{8}$

8. $9 + 2 = \underline{11}$

Do the Math

Skill **8**

Use the number line to add. Write the sum.

1. Liz has 5 marbles. She gets 3 more. How many marbles does Liz have now?

Remember
Make jumps to the right to add.

- Which is the greater number? $\underline{5}$
- How many will you count on? $\underline{3}$
- $5 + 3 = \underline{8}$

So, Liz has $\underline{8}$ marbles now.

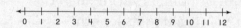

2. $7 + 2 = \underline{9}$

3. $2 + 5 = \underline{7}$

4. $6 + 3 = \underline{9}$

5. $3 + 7 = \underline{10}$

6. $2 + 9 = \underline{11}$

7. $2 + 6 = \underline{8}$

8. $4 + 1 = \underline{5}$

9. $3 + 8 = \underline{11}$

10. $1 + 9 = \underline{10}$

11. $1 + 11 = \underline{12}$

12. There are 4 birds in a tree. 2 more birds join them. How many birds are there in all? $\underline{6}$ birds

Name _____

Learn the Math

Use a number line to count on.

- What is $7 + 3$?

- Start on the greater number.

- Make jumps to the right.

- Write the sum.

© Houghton Mifflin Harcourt Publishing Company

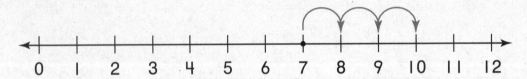

So, $7 + 3 =$ ____.

Use the number line to add. Write each sum.

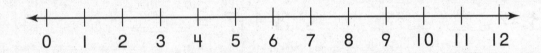

1. $4 + 3 =$ ____

2. $8 + 2 =$ ____

3. $5 + 1 =$ ____

4. $3 + 9 =$ ____

5. $6 + 1 =$ ____

6. $2 + 7 =$ ____

7. $3 + 5 =$ ____

8. $9 + 2 =$ ____

Vocabulary

number line
count on

Use the number line to add. Write the sum.

1. Liz has 5 marbles. She gets 3 more. How many marbles does Liz have now?

Remember

Make jumps to the right to add.

· Which is the greater number? _____

· How many will you count on? _____

· $5 + 3 =$ _____

So, Liz has _____ marbles now.

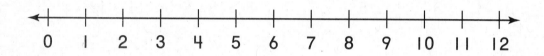

0 1 2 3 4 5 6 7 8 9 10 11 12

2. $7 + 2 =$ _____ | **3.** $2 + 5 =$ _____

4. $6 + 3 =$ _____ | **5.** $3 + 7 =$ _____

6. $2 + 9 =$ _____ | **7.** $2 + 6 =$ _____

8. $4 + 1 =$ _____ | **9.** $3 + 8 =$ _____

10. $1 + 9 =$ _____ | **11.** $1 + 11 =$ _____

12. There are 4 birds in a tree. 2 more birds join them. How many birds are there in all?   _____ birds

Objective
To use a number line to count back to find differences

Vocabulary
count back To count backward from a given number

COMMON ERROR

- Children may count on instead of counting back.
- To correct this, remind children to count to the left on the number line.

Learn the Math page IN35 Discuss the number line with children. Point out that to count back, or subtract, they must move to the left. If children have difficulty remembering which is left, point out that the numbers get smaller as they move in that direction.

Instruct children to place their finger on the 10 on the number line to model the first step. Ask: **What number are you starting with?** 10 Demonstrate for children how to move their fingers to the left on the number line to count back. Suggest that they whisper, "10," and then say "9, 8, 7" in their normal voices as they count back three in Step 2. Guide children through Step 3.

REASONING Ask: **Why do you move to the left on a number line when you subtract?** Possible answer: the numbers get smaller when you move to the left.

Do the Math page IN36 Read and discuss Exercise 1 with children. Guide them to identify the numbers in the subtraction problem. Encourage them to count out loud as they count back to solve the subtraction sentence.

Assign Exercises 2–11 and monitor children's work.

Read Problem 12 with children. Encourage them to use a number line. Have them start with the greater number and count back to find how many children are left.

Children who make more than 3 errors in Exercises 1–12 may benefit from the **Alternative Teaching Strategy**.

Alternative Teaching Strategy
Manipulatives and Materials: connecting cubes, number lines 0–12 (see *Teacher Resources*)

Have children use connecting cubes to count back on a number line. Write a problem on the board that involves subtracting 1, 2, or 3; such as $11 - 3 =$ _____. Give each child a number line and 3 connecting cubes. To count back 3, have children place a cube above 10, above 9, and above 8 on a number line. The difference, 8, is the last cube placed on the number line.

Name _____

Learn the Math

Use a number line to count back.

What is 10 − 3?

Vocabulary

count back

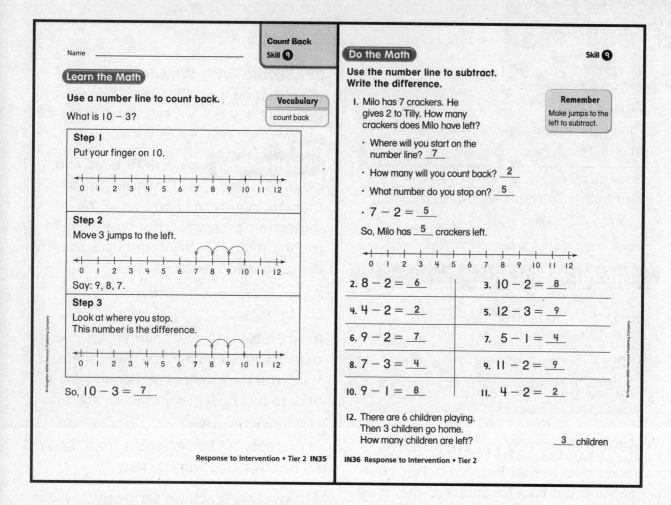

Step 1
Put your finger on 10.

0 1 2 3 4 5 6 7 8 9 10 11 12

Step 2
Move 3 jumps to the left.

0 1 2 3 4 5 6 7 8 9 10 11 12

Say: 9, 8, 7.

Step 3
Look at where you stop.
This number is the difference.

0 1 2 3 4 5 6 7 8 9 10 11 12

So, 10 − 3 = __7__.

Do the Math

Skill **9**

Use the number line to subtract.
Write the difference.

Remember
Make jumps to the left to subtract.

1. Milo has 7 crackers. He gives 2 to Tilly. How many crackers does Milo have left?

· Where will you start on the number line? __7__

· How many will you count back? __2__

· What number do you stop on? __5__

· 7 − 2 = __5__

So, Milo has __5__ crackers left.

0 1 2 3 4 5 6 7 8 9 10 11 12

2. 8 − 2 = __6__   3. 10 − 2 = __8__

4. 4 − 2 = __2__   5. 12 − 3 = __9__

6. 9 − 2 = __7__   7. 5 − 1 = __4__

8. 7 − 3 = __4__   9. 11 − 2 = __9__

10. 9 − 1 = __8__   11. 4 − 2 = __2__

12. There are 6 children playing. Then 3 children go home. How many children are left?   __3__ children

Name _____

Learn the Math

Use a number line to count back.

What is 10 − 3?

Vocabulary

count back

Step 1

Put your finger on 10.

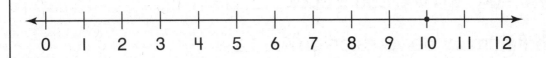

Step 2

Move 3 jumps to the left.

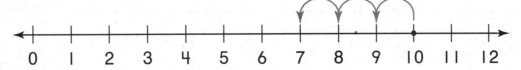

Say: 9, 8, 7.

Step 3

Look at where you stop.
This number is the difference.

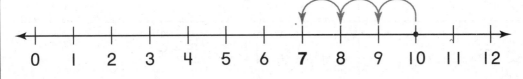

So, 10 − 3 = ___.

**Use the number line to subtract.
Write the difference.**

I. Milo has 7 crackers. He gives 2 to Tilly. How many crackers does Milo have left?

- Where will you start on the number line? ____

- How many will you count back? ____

- What number do you stop on? ____

- $7 - 2 =$ ____

So, Milo has ____ crackers left.

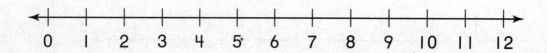

2. $8 - 2 =$ ____

3. $10 - 2 =$ ____

4. $4 - 2 =$ ____

5. $12 - 3 =$ ____

6. $9 - 2 =$ ____

7. $5 - 1 =$ ____

8. $7 - 3 =$ ____

9. $11 - 2 =$ ____

10. $9 - 1 =$ ____

11. $4 - 2 =$ ____

12. There are 6 children playing.
Then 3 children go home.
How many children are left?

____ children

Count Groups to 20

Skill 10

Objective
To count groups of up to 20 objects

Manipulatives and Materials
counters, ten frames (see *Teacher Resources*)

COMMON ERROR

- Children may try to count a group of 10 as individual objects.

- To correct this, remind children to count a group of 10 as a whole group.

Learn the Math page IN39 Read and work through the example with children. Ask: **How many groups of 10 are there?** 1 group of 10 Remind children that when they see a group of 10 objects, they do not need to count each item individually.

Discuss with children how they can first count the group of 10, and then count the rest of the objects to find the total number in the group. Work through Exercises 1–4 with children. Ask: **How can you count the groups in Exercise 1?** Possible answer: I can count a group of 10 and then count on from 10: 10, 11, 12, 13, 14, 15.

REASONING Have children use ten frames and counters to find how many groups of 10 counters are needed to make 20. Ask: **How many groups of 10 counters would you need to make 20?** 2 groups of 10 counters

Discuss with children why organizing each group of 10 in the same way (i.e., setting up 2 rows each with 5 counters for each group of 10) helps them count the number in each group.

Do the Math page IN40 Read and discuss Exercise 1 with children. Guide them to solve the problem. Encourage children to count the group of 10 as a ten, rather than count each object individually.

Assign Exercises 2–5 and monitor children's work.

Have children model Problem 6 with counters and ten frames. Check that children first make a group of 10. Remind them to include in their count the 2 counters that are not in the group of 10.

Children who make more than 1 error in Exercises 1–6 may benefit from the **Alternative Teaching Strategy**.

Alternative Teaching Strategy
Manipulatives and Materials: counters, ten frames (see *Teacher Resources*)

Have partners use ten frames to model numbers to 20. Give each child an index card with a number on it. Have one partner model the number on ten frames using counters. Then have the other partner count the objects in the groups and name the number. Have children trade roles and repeat the activity.

Name _____

Learn the Math

You can count numbers in groups.
How many are in the group?

Step 1	
Count the counters.	Count a group of 10 first.
Step 2	
Say the number.	THINK: nineteen
Step 3	
Write the number.	19

Count the ⬤. Write the number.

1. 15

2. 13

3. 16

4. 12

Response to Intervention • Tier 2 **IN39**

Do the Math

Count each object. Write how many.

1.

- How many groups of 10 🐟 are there? __1__ group of 10 🐟
- How many other 🐟 are there? __7__ 🐟
- How many 🐟 are there in all? __17__

So, there are __17__ 🐟 in the group.

> **Remember**
> · Count a group of 10 first.
> · Then count the rest.

2. 18

3. 14

Circle groups of 10. Write how many.

4. 20

5. 13

6. Karen has 1 group of 10 stamps. Dashel has 2 stamps. How many stamps do Karen and Dashel have in all? __12__ stamps

IN40 Response to Intervention • Tier 2

Name _____

Learn the Math

You can count numbers in groups.
How many are in the group?

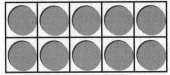 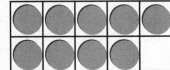

Step 1 Count the counters.	Count a group of 10 first.
Step 2 Say the number.	THINK: nineteen
Step 3 Write the number.	19

Count the ⬤. Write the number.

1.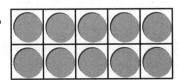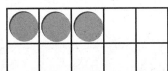

_____

2.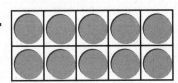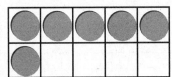

_____

3.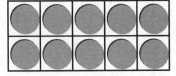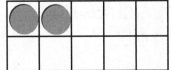

_____

4.

_____

Count each object. Write how many.

1.

- How many groups of 10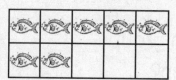
  are there? _____ group of 10

- How many other 🐟 are
  there? _____

- How many 🐟 are there in all? _____

So, there are _____ 🐟 in the group.

2.

3.

Circle groups of 10. Write how many.

4. _____

_____

5. _____

_____

6. Karen has 1 group of 10 stamps. Dashel
   has 2 stamps. How many stamps do
   Karen and Dashel have in all?

   _____ stamps

Objective
To model different ways to show a group of 10

Manipulatives
two-color counters, color tiles

COMMON ERROR

- Children may skip an object or a picture as they count.

- To correct this, have children use two-color counters to model groups of 10 and then turn the counters over as they count the group.

Learn the Math page IN43 Distribute 10 counters to each child. Have them explore ways to arrange a group of 10 counters. Guide children through the examples on the page. Ask: **How many counters are in Example 1?** 10 counters Then elicit from children that there are 10 counters in each of the next two examples. Guide children to notice that the arrangement of the counters does not change the number of counters in the group. Explain to children that for Exercises 1 and 2 they should draw enough circles to show a group of 10.

REASONING Ask: **How can you arrange your counters so that it is easy to see a group of 10?** Accept reasonable answers. Check that children can demonstrate a group that is easy to distinguish as a group of 10.

Do the Math page IN44 Guide children through Exercise 1. Remind them that there are many different ways to show a group of 10.

Assign Exercises 2–5 and monitor children's work.

Children may wish to model Problem 6 with color tiles before they draw the tiles needed to make a group of 10. Encourage them to show a way that is different from the other ways on the page.

Children who make more than 1 error in Exercises 1–6 may benefit from the **Alternative Teaching Strategy.**

Alternative Teaching Strategy
Materials: paper bag, 10 of the same kind of small classroom objects, paper

Have partners use a bag of 10 objects to model a group of 10. Direct one partner to take a few objects from the bag, arrange them in a group, and count the number of objects. Have the second partner remove one object at a time from the bag and count to complete the group of 10. Have partners draw the group of 10 and write the number below the drawing.

Learn the Math

You can show a group of 10 in different ways.

Example 1 Use ●. Show one way.	● ● ● ● ● ● ● ● ● ●
Example 2 Show another way.	● ● ● ● ● ● ● ● ● ●
Example 3 These are different ways to show a group of 10.	● ● ● ● ● ● ● ● ● ●

Use ●. Draw to show a group of 10. **Arrangements may vary.**

1. ● ● ● ● ● ● ● ○ ○ ○

2. ● ● ● ● ● ● ○ ○ ○ ○

Do the Math

Use ●. Draw to show a group of 10.

Arrangements may vary for Exercises 1–6.

Remember
You can show a group of 10 in different ways.

1. ● ● ● ● ○ ○
   ○ ○ ○ ○

   · How many ● do you need in all? __10__ counters
   · Count the ● in the group. __4__ counters
   · How many ○ should you draw? __6__ counters

2. ● ● ● ● ●
   ● ● ●
   ○ ○

3. ● ● ○ ○
   ● ● ● ○ ○ ○

Use ●. Draw to show a group of 10 in two different ways.

4. ○ ○ ○ ○
   ○ ○ ○
   ○ ○ ○

5. ○ ○   ○ ○
   ○ ○ ○   ○ ○ ○
   ○ ○   ○ ○

6. Ben makes a group of 10 tiles. Draw a group Ben might make.

   ▢ ▢ ▢ ◼ ◼
   ▢ ▢ ▢ ▢ ▢

Name _____

Learn the Math

You can show a group of 10 in different ways.

Example 1 Use ⚪. Show one way.	
Example 2 Show another way.	
Example 3 These are different ways to show a group of 10.	

Use ⚪. Draw to show a group of 10.

1.	2.

Use ⬤ **. Draw to show a group of 10.**

1. ⬤ ⬤ ⬤ ⬤

- How many ⬤ do you need in all? ＿＿ counters
- Count the ⬤ in the group. ＿＿ counters
- How many ⬤ should you draw? ＿＿ counters

2. ⬤ ⬤ ⬤ ⬤ ⬤
   ⬤ ⬤ ⬤

3. ⬤ ⬤
   ⬤ ⬤ ⬤

Use ⬤ **. Draw to show a group of 10 in two different ways.**

4.

5.

6. Ben makes a group of 10 tiles. Draw a group Ben might make.

Objective
To create sets that have more or fewer objects

Manipulatives and Materials
counters, crayons

COMMON ERROR

- Children may not understand whether they should have a greater number of objects or a fewer number of objects than the pictures provided.

- To correct this, demonstrate and model how to use counters to show more or fewer.

Learn the Math page IN47 Read the example with children. Tell them to place one counter beneath each picture so that the set of counters shows more. Ask: **How do you know that the set of counters shows more?** Possible answer: there are 3 dogs and 4 counters. 4 is one more than 3. Point out Exercise 1 to children. Ask: **How many fish are there?** 4 fish **How many counters do you need to show fewer?** Possible answers: 3, 2, or 1 counters Have children draw the counters needed to show fewer.

REASONING Ask: **How can you tell that your set shows fewer?** Possible answer: I can count the number of pictures in the first set and then make a set with one less.

Do the Math page IN48 On this page, children color boxes rather than placing counters. For children who have difficulty, draw bigger frames and allow them to use counters. For other children, you might have them circle the key words: *more* and *fewer*. Guide children to solve Exercise 1. Help children count the pictures and then help them count the boxes they colored.

Assign Exercises 2–5 and monitor children's work.

For Problem 6, encourage children to use counters to represent the books Nick and Sal have. Elicit from children that 2 fewer than 5 books is 3 books. Have them color the squares to show their work.

Children who make more than 1 error in Exercises 1–6 may benefit from the **Alternative Teaching Strategy.**

Alternative Teaching Strategy
Manipulatives and Materials: connecting cubes, numeral cards (see *Teacher Resources*)

Have partners place the numeral cards facedown in a pile. Have the first partner choose a card and build a cube train for that number. Have the second partner build a cube train that is more than that number. Encourage children to repeat the activity to show a set of fewer.

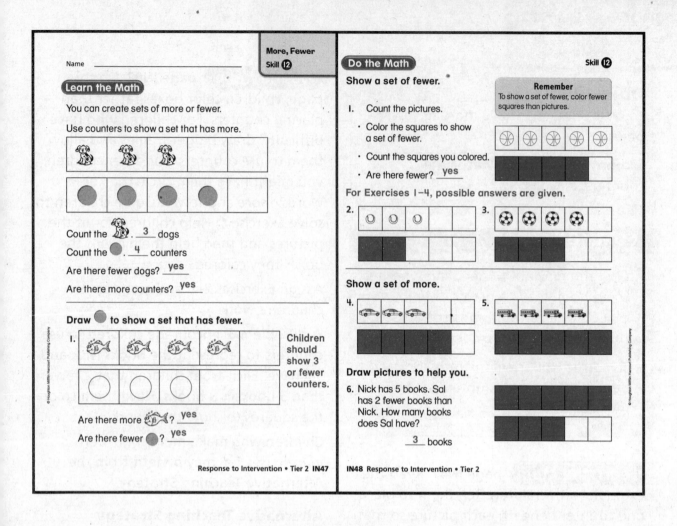

Name _____

Learn the Math

You can create sets of more or fewer.

Use counters to show a set that has more.

Count the 🐕. __3__ dogs

Count the ⬤. __4__ counters

Are there fewer dogs? __yes__

Are there more counters? __yes__

Draw ⬤ to show a set that has fewer.

1.

Children should show 3 or fewer counters.

Are there more 🐟? __yes__

Are there fewer ⬤? __yes__

Do the Math

Skill 12

Show a set of fewer.

Remember
To show a set of fewer, color fewer squares than pictures.

1. Count the pictures.
   - Color the squares to show a set of fewer.
   - Count the squares you colored.
   - Are there fewer? __yes__

For Exercises 1–4, possible answers are given.

2.

3.

Show a set of more.

4.

5.

Draw pictures to help you.

6. Nick has 5 books. Sal has 2 fewer books than Nick. How many books does Sal have?

   __3__ books

Learn the Math

You can create sets of more or fewer.

Use counters to show a set that has more.

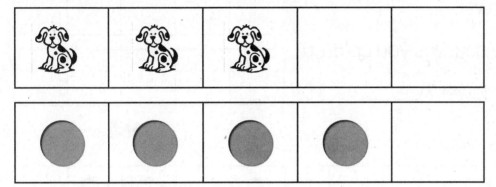

Count the 🐕 . _____ dogs

Count the ⬤ . _____ counters

Are there fewer dogs? _____

Are there more counters? _____

Draw ⬤ to show a set that has fewer.

1.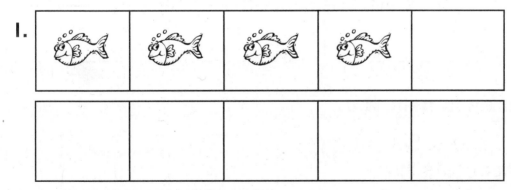

Are there more 🐟 ? _____

Are there fewer ⬤ ? _____

Do the Math

Show a set of fewer.

1. Count the pictures.

    · Color the squares to show a set of fewer.

    · Count the squares you colored.

    · Are there fewer? _____

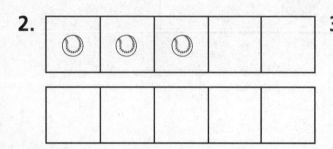

2.

3.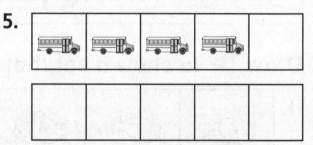

Show a set of more.

4.

5.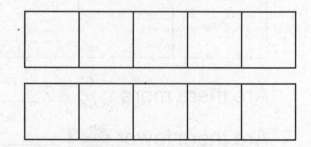

Draw pictures to help you.

6. Nick has 5 books. Sal has 2 fewer books than Nick. How many books does Sal have?

    _____ books

Draw Equal Groups

Skill 13

Objective
To create sets that have the same number of objects

Manipulatives and Materials
counters, crayons

COMMON ERROR

- Children may not understand that they should have the same number of objects in each set.

- To correct this, demonstrate and model how to use counters and one-to-one correspondence to make equal sets.

Learn the Math page IN51 Read the example with children. Tell them to place one counter beneath each picture to create a set with the same number of objects as the set of apples. Ask: **How many apples are there?** 4 apples **How many counters did you show?** 4 counters

Have children count the number of bananas in Exercise 1. Ask: **How many counters will you show?** 3 counters Have children draw a counter below each picture. Ask: **How can you tell if the sets have the same number of objects?** Possible answers: I can count the number of objects in each set and compare; I can match one counter and one picture from each set and compare.

REASONING Ask: How can you tell without counting that one set has the same number of objects as another set? Possible answer: there are no objects left over after matching them.

Do the Math page IN52 On this page, children color boxes rather than place counters. Some children may wish to use counters to represent the pictures and the sets they make. Guide children to solve Exercise 1. Help children count the pictures and then help them count the boxes they colored. Point out to children that there are the same number of each.

Assign Exercises 2–5 and monitor children's work.

For Problem 6, encourage children to use counters to represent the forks and spoons. Elicit that Kiana has 3 forks, so she will need 3 spoons. Have children draw to show their work.

Children who make more than 1 error in Exercises 1–6 may benefit from the **Alternative Teaching Strategy.**

Alternative Teaching Strategy
Have children act out sets of the same number. Invite three volunteers to stand. Then ask three more volunteers to stand, one at a time, and be a "partner" to one of the volunteers in the first set. When all volunteers are standing, have children count the first set of three and then count the second set of three. Review that each of the sets have the same number of children.

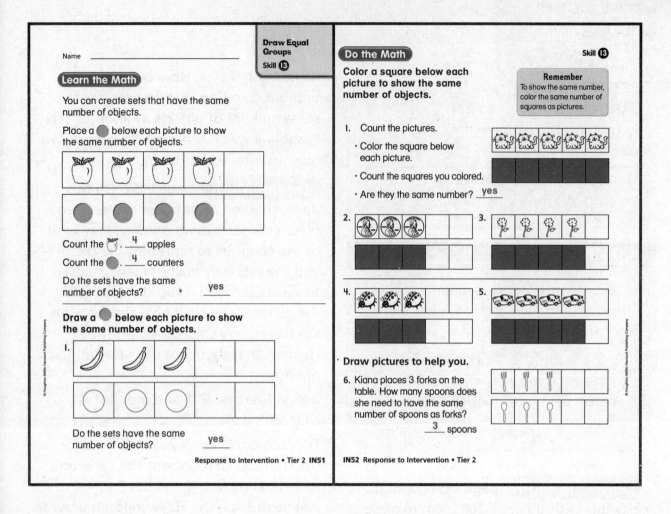

Learn the Math

You can create sets that have the same number of objects.

Place a ⬤ below each picture to show the same number of objects.

Count the 🍎. __4__ apples

Count the ⬤. __4__ counters

Do the sets have the same number of objects?   __yes__

Draw a ⬤ below each picture to show the same number of objects.

1.

Do the sets have the same number of objects?   __yes__

Do the Math

Color a square below each picture to show the same number of objects.

> **Remember**
> To show the same number, color the same number of squares as pictures.

1. Count the pictures.
   · Color the square below each picture.
   · Count the squares you colored.
   · Are they the same number? __yes__

2.   3.

4.   5.

Draw pictures to help you.

6. Kiana places 3 forks on the table. How many spoons does she need to have the same number of spoons as forks?

   __3__ spoons

Name _____

Learn the Math

You can create sets that have the same number of objects.

Place a 🔵 below each picture to show the same number of objects.

Count the 🍎 . _____ apples

Count the 🔵 . _____ counters

Do the sets have the same
number of objects?   _____

**Draw a 🔵 below each picture to show
the same number of objects.**

I.

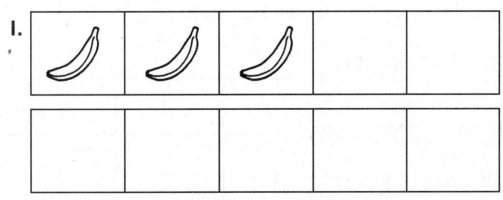

Do the sets have the same
number of objects?   _____

Do the Math

Color a square below each picture to show the same number of objects.

1. Count the pictures.

   • Color the square below each picture.

   • Count the squares you colored.

   • Are they the same number? _____

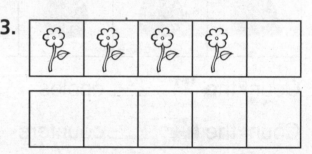

2.

3.

4.

5.

Draw pictures to help you.

6. Kiana places 3 forks on the table. How many spoons does she need to have the same number of spoons as forks?

   _____ spoons

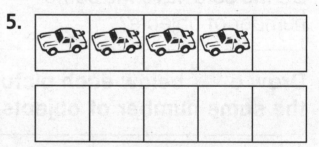

Objective
To use a number line to order numbers from least to greatest

Vocabulary
least fewest in quantity or amount
greatest largest in size, or most in quantity or amount

COMMON ERROR

- Children may get confused about least and greatest.

- To correct this, review the terms using manipulatives so children can visualize the meaning of each term.

Learn the Math page IN55 Read and discuss the example with children. Use the number line to explain to children the meanings of *least* and *greatest*. Have them find each of the three numbers on the number line and then write them in order from least to greatest. Ask: **How does the number line help you put the numbers in order?** Possible answer: the numbers on the number line are in order. I can find these numbers on the number line and then put them in the same order.

Work through Exercises 1–4 with children. Remind them to use the number line to locate and order the numbers. Check that children write all three numbers in order from least to greatest.

REASONING Ask: Suppose Lana says that 43 is greater than 44 and 46. Do you agree? No; possible answer: if I look on a number line, I see that 43 is less than 44 and 46. Use a number line to demonstrate how to find the answer.

Do the Math page IN56 Read and discuss Exercise 1 with children. Guide them to solve the problem. Ask: **How do you order numbers from least to greatest?** Possible answer: the least number is first, and the greatest number is last.

Assign Exercises 2–5 and monitor children's work.

For Problem 6, have children use the number line in Exercise 1 to help them solve the problem. Have them write the names in order from the child with the least number of beads to the child with the greatest number of beads.

Children who make more than 1 error in Exercises 1–6 may benefit from the **Alternative Teaching Strategy.**

Alternative Teaching Strategy
Manipulatives: connecting cubes

Have children use cube trains to help them visualize the size of numbers as numbers are ordered. Give partners three sets of cube trains. Have them arrange the sets in order from the least amount to the greatest amount. Ask one partner to count the number of cubes in each train while the other partner writes the numbers in order from least to greatest.

Name _____

Learn the Math

You can use a number line to order numbers.

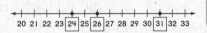

Order these numbers from least to greatest.

    24   31   26

Find these numbers on the number line.

- Which number is first? __24__
- Which number is second? __26__
- Which number is third? __31__

Order the numbers from least to greatest.

__24__   __26__   __31__

Use the number line. Write the numbers in order from least to greatest.

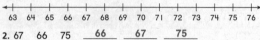

1. 47 45 53   __45__   __47__   __53__
2. 42 50 46   __42__   __46__   __50__
3. 49 54 44   __44__   __49__   __54__
4. 55 51 48   __48__   __51__   __55__

Do the Math

Use the number line. Write the numbers in order from least to greatest.

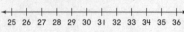

1. 32 35 27

- Which number is first? __27__
- Which number is second? __32__
- Which number is third? __35__

Order the numbers from least to greatest.

__27__   __32__   __35__

Remember

As you move from left to right on the number line, the numbers are greater.

Use the number line. Write the numbers in order from least to greatest.

2. 67 66 75   __66__   __67__   __75__
3. 64 72 68   __64__   __68__   __72__
4. 76 63 65   __63__   __65__   __76__
5. 70 73 69   __69__   __70__   __73__

Write the names in order from who has the least to who has the greatest number of beads.

6. Yolanda has 31 beads. Marita has 29 beads. Rico has 36 beads.

__Marita__   __Yolanda__   __Rico__

Name _____

Learn the Math

You can use a number line to order numbers.

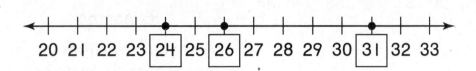

Order these numbers from least to greatest.

24   31   26

Find these numbers on the number line.

· Which number is first? _____

· Which number is second? _____

· Which number is third? _____

Order the numbers from least to greatest.

_____ _____ _____

Use the number line. Write the numbers in order from least to greatest.

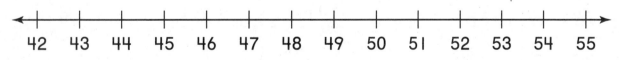

1. 47   45   53   _____ _____ _____

2. 42   50   46   _____ _____ _____

3. 49   54   44   _____ _____ _____

4. 55   51   48   _____ _____ _____

Use the number line. Write the numbers in order from least to greatest.

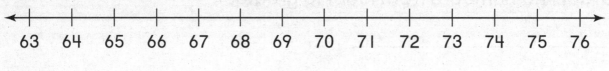

25 26 27 28 29 30 31 32 33 34 35 36

> **Remember**
> As you move from left to right on the number line, the numbers are greater.

1. 32   35   27

- Which number is first? _____
- Which number is second? _____
- Which number is third? _____

Order the numbers from least to greatest.

_____ _____ _____

Use the number line. Write the numbers in order from least to greatest.

63 64 65 66 67 68 69 70 71 72 73 74 75 76

2. 67   66   75   _____ _____ _____

3. 64   72   68   _____ _____ _____

4. 76   63   65   _____ _____ _____

5. 70   73   69   _____ _____ _____

Write the names in order from who has the least to who has the greatest number of beads.

6. Yolanda has 31 beads. Marita has 29 beads. Rico has 36 beads.

_____ _____ _____

Objective
To count forward using a hundred chart

Materials
crayons, hundred chart (see *Teacher Resources*)

COMMON ERROR

- Children may make counting errors as they move from one row to the next on the hundred chart.

- To correct this, explain to children how to read the numbers from left to right and from top to bottom.

Learn the Math page IN59 Distribute a hundred chart to each child and allow children to become familiar with it. Ask such questions as: **How is the hundred chart organized? What is the same in each row? What is the same in each column? How is each row or column different?** Guide children through the first example. Remind them to touch each number as it is counted. For the second example, explain to children that this problem does not start on number 1, but instead starts on number 46. Ask: **What is the last number you counted?** 59 Check that children color the box for the number 59.

REASONING Say: Suppose Ben starts at 26 and counts to 39 on the hundred chart. Ask: **If Ben colors the box for 40, is he correct? Explain.** Possible answer: he is not correct, because he should have colored the box for 39.

Do the Math page IN60 Read and discuss Exercise 1 with children. Explain that to count to 18 also means to stop on 18. Remind children to color the last number counted.

Assign Exercises 2–9 and monitor children's work.

For Problem 10, encourage children to use the hundred chart to help them circle the numbers Pam counts.

Children who make more than 2 errors in Exercises 1–10 may benefit from the **Alternative Teaching Strategy.**

Alternative Teaching Strategy
Materials: hundred chart (see *Teacher Resources*)

Prepare cutouts of number sequences taken from a hundred chart for partners to count. Have the first partner use the cutout number sequence to count the sequence. Then have the second partner place the cutout in the correct position on a complete hundred chart and count the sequence. Invite partners to select a new sequence and switch roles.

Learn the Math

You can use a hundred chart to count.

Example 1

Start at 1 and count to 23.

- Start at 1.
  Touch and count.
- Stop at 23.
- Color the last number you counted.

1	2	3	4	5	6	7	8	9	10
11	12	13	14	15	16	17	18	19	20
21	22	23	24	25	26	27	28	29	30
31	32	33	34	35	36	37	38	39	40
41	42	43	44	45	46	47	48	49	50
51	52	53	54	55	56	57	58	59	60
61	62	63	64	65	66	67	68	69	70
71	72	73	74	75	76	77	78	79	80
81	82	83	84	85	86	87	88	89	90
91	92	93	94	95	96	97	98	99	100

Example 2

Start at 46 and count to 59.

- Start at 46.
  Touch and count.
- Stop at 59.
- Color the last number you counted.

1	2	3	4	5	6	7	8	9	10
11	12	13	14	15	16	17	18	19	20
21	22	23	24	25	26	27	28	29	30
31	32	33	34	35	36	37	38	39	40
41	42	43	44	45	46	47	48	49	50
51	52	53	54	55	56	57	58	59	60
61	62	63	64	65	66	67	68	69	70
71	72	73	74	75	76	77	78	79	80
81	82	83	84	85	86	87	88	89	90
91	92	93	94	95	96	97	98	99	100

Do the Math

Skill 15

Touch and count. Color the last number counted.

> **Remember**
> Touch each number as you count.

1. Start at 3 and count to 18.
   - Start at 3.
   - Touch and count.
   - Stop at 18.
   - Color the last number you counted.

2. Start at 20 and count to 33.

3. Start at 36 and count to 49.

4. Start at 51 and count to 62.

5. Start at 68 and count to 85.

6. Start at 87 and count to 98.

1	2	3	4	5	6	7	8	9	10
11	12	13	14	15	16	17	18	19	20
21	22	23	24	25	26	27	28	29	30
31	32	33	34	35	36	37	38	39	40
41	42	43	44	45	46	47	48	49	50
51	52	53	54	55	56	57	58	59	60
61	62	63	64	65	66	67	68	69	70
71	72	73	74	75	76	77	78	79	80
81	82	83	84	85	86	87	88	89	90
91	92	93	94	95	96	97	98	99	100

Use the hundred chart. Write the missing numbers.

7. 64, 65, __66__, __67__, 68, __69__, 70, __71__

8. 72, 73, __74__, 75, __76__, __77__, 78, __79__

9. 58, 59, __60__, __61__, 62, 63, __64__, __65__

Use the hundred chart.

10. Pam counts to 79. She starts at 66.
    Circle the numbers she counts.

    80   (76)   65   (73)   63   86   (69)

Name _____

Learn the Math

You can use a hundred chart to count.

Example 1

**Start at 1 and count
to 23.**

- Start at 1.
  Touch and count.

- Stop at 23.

- Color the last number
  you counted.

1	2	3	4	5	6	7	8	9	10
11	12	13	14	15	16	17	18	19	20
21	22	23	24	25	26	27	28	29	30
31	32	33	34	35	36	37	38	39	40
41	42	43	44	45	46	47	48	49	50
51	52	53	54	55	56	57	58	59	60
61	62	63	64	65	66	67	68	69	70
71	72	73	74	75	76	77	78	79	80
81	82	83	84	85	86	87	88	89	90
91	92	93	94	95	96	97	98	99	100

Example 2

**Start at 46 and count
to 59.**

- Start at 46.
  Touch and count.

- Stop at 59.

- Color the last number
  you counted.

1	2	3	4	5	6	7	8	9	10
11	12	13	14	15	16	17	18	19	20
21	22	23	24	25	26	27	28	29	30
31	32	33	34	35	36	37	38	39	40
41	42	43	44	45	46	47	48	49	50
51	52	53	54	55	56	57	58	59	60
61	62	63	64	65	66	67	68	69	70
71	72	73	74	75	76	77	78	79	80
81	82	83	84	85	86	87	88	89	90
91	92	93	94	95	96	97	98	99	100

Touch and count. Color the last number counted.

1. Start at 3 and count to 18.

   - Start at 3.

   - Touch and count.

   - Stop at 18.

   - Color the last number you counted.

1	2	3	4	5	6	7	8	9	10
11	12	13	14	15	16	17	18	19	20
21	22	23	24	25	26	27	28	29	30
31	32	33	34	35	36	37	38	39	40
41	42	43	44	45	46	47	48	49	50
51	52	53	54	55	56	57	58	59	60
61	62	63	64	65	66	67	68	69	70
71	72	73	74	75	76	77	78	79	80
81	82	83	84	85	86	87	88	89	90
91	92	93	94	95	96	97	98	99	100

2. Start at 20 and count to 33.

3. Start at 36 and count to 49.

4. Start at 51 and count to 62.

5. Start at 68 and count to 85.

6. Start at 87 and count to 98.

Use the hundred chart. Write the missing numbers.

7. 64, 65, _____ , _____ , 68, _____ , 70, _____

8. 72, 73, _____ , 75, _____ , _____ , 78, _____

9. 58, 59, _____ , _____ , 62, 63, _____ , _____

Use the hundred chart.

10. Pam counts to 79. She starts at 66.
    Circle the numbers she counts.

    80   76   65   73   63   86   69

Read Picture Graphs
Skill 16

Objective
To use information from a picture graph to answer questions

COMMON ERROR

- Children may not understand what information they are looking at when reading a picture graph.

- To correct this, model how to read the title of the picture graph and how to read all of the labels.

Learn the Math page IN63 Discuss the parts of the picture graph with children. Then point out the question about the graph. Ask: **What does the question ask you to find?** the toy the most children like

Read Step 2 aloud. Ask: **How can you find how many children like each type of toy?** I can count the number of smiley faces in each row.

In Step 3, guide children to compare the numbers from Step 2. Ask: **How does comparing the numbers help you answer the question?** The toy with the greatest number is the toy most children like.

REASONING Say: **Looking at the picture graph, Sarah says that 7 children chose yo-yos.** Ask: **Do you agree?** Possible answer: I do not agree. The graph only shows 6 smiley faces, so 6 children chose yo-yos, not 7. Discuss the problem.

Do the Math page IN64 Look at the picture graph with children. Guide children through reading the title of the graph. Ask: **Is this graph about dogs?** No; it is about sports. **How do you know?** The title of the graph and the labels in the graph are about sports. Guide children to answer the questions. Ask: **Which row shows the number of children who chose basketball?** Children should point to the row with the basketball.

Assign Exercises 2–3 and monitor children's work.

For Problem 4, ask: **How does the picture graph help you answer the question?** Possible answer: the pictures in the picture graph show which choice has the most without having to count.

Children who make more than 1 error in Exercises 1–4 may benefit from the **Alternative Teaching Strategy.**

Alternative Teaching Strategy

On the board, draw a three-row graph grid titled "Colors of Cubes in a Bag" with six smiley faces in the top row, 5 smiley faces in the middle row, and 8 smiley faces in the bottom row. Label the rows from top to bottom as red, blue, yellow.

Ask how many there are of each color, and which colors are recorded least and most. Have children explain how they can tell.

Name _____

Learn the Math

You can use the picture graph to answer questions.

The picture graph shows the favorite toys of the children in Jim's class.

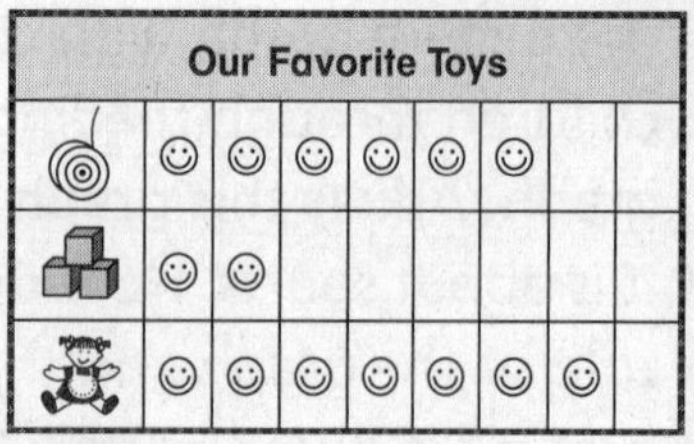

Our Favorite Toys						
🎯	☺	☺	☺	☺	☺	
🧱	☺	☺				
🧸	☺	☺	☺	☺	☺	☺

Which toy do the most children like?

Step 1 Read the question.	Which toy do the most children like?
Step 2 Write how many children like each type of toy.	🎯 🧱 🧸 6 2 7
Step 3 Circle the toy that the most children like.	🎯 🧱 (🧸)

So, the most children like 🧸.

Response to Intervention • Tier 2 **IN63**

Do the Math

Use the picture graph.

Sports We Like						
🏀	🧍	🧍	🧍			
🌙	🧍	🧍	🧍	🧍	🧍	🧍
⚽	🧍	🧍	🧍	🧍		

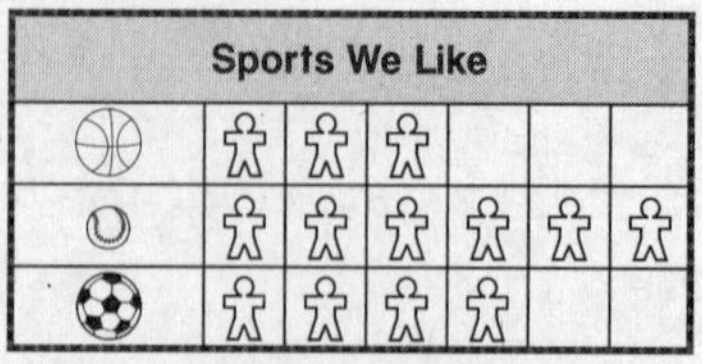

Remember
Read the title and the labels on the picture graph first.

1. Which sport do the fewest children like?
   - How many children chose 🏀 ? _3_
   - How many children chose 🌙 ? _6_
   - How many children chose ⚽ ? _4_

   Circle the sport the fewest children like.   (🏀)   🌙   ⚽

Use the picture graph.

How We Get to School						
🚌	☺	☺	☺	☺	☺	☺ ☺
🚗	☺	☺	☺			
🚶	☺	☺	☺	☺	☺	

2. How many children 🚶 ? _5_
3. How many children ride the 🚌 ? _7_
4. How do the most children get to school? Explain.
   Bus; Possible answer: There are 7 boxes filled for
   bus, and only 3 for car and 5 for walk.

IN64 Response to Intervention • Tier 2

Name _____

Learn the Math

You can use the picture graph to answer questions.

The picture graph shows the favorite toys of the children in Jim's class.

Our Favorite Toys								
◎	☺	☺	☺	☺	☺	☺		
🧊	☺	☺						
👧	☺	☺	☺	☺	☺	☺	☺	

Which toy do the most children like?

Step 1 Read the question.	Which toy do the most children like?
Step 2 Write how many children like each type of toy.	◎ 🧊 👧 ____ ____ ____
Step 3 Circle the toy that the most children like.	◎ 🧊 👧

So, the most children like .

Use the picture graph.

Sports We Like					
🏀	👤	👤	👤		
⚾	👤	👤	👤	👤	👤	👤
⚽	👤	👤	👤	👤	

1. Which sport do the fewest children like?

   · How many children chose 🏀 ? _____

   · How many children chose ⚾ ? _____

   · How many children chose ⚽ ? _____

   Circle the sport the fewest children like.   🏀 ⚾ ⚽

Use the picture graph.

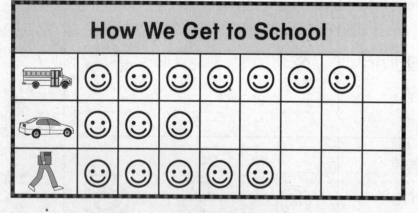

How We Get to School							
🚌	🙂	🙂	🙂	🙂	🙂	🙂	🙂
🚗	🙂	🙂	🙂				
🚶	🙂	🙂	🙂	🙂	🙂		

2. How many children 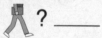 ? _____

3. How many children ride the 🚌 ? _____

4. How do the most children get to school? Explain.

   _____

   _____

Objective
To use data from a picture graph to solve problems

COMMON ERROR

- Children may count the number of pictures in one row of a picture graph incorrectly.

- To correct this, show children how to track across a row and count each picture in the row.

Learn the Math page IN67 Read and discuss the food picture graph with children. Show how to count the number of pictures in each row, reminding them that each picture represents one.

Instruct children to look at the first row of the graph. Ask: **How many smiley face pictures are in the first row?** 3 Say: **If there are 3 smiley face pictures in the row, then 3 children like hot dogs best.** Repeat with the rows for hamburger and pizza. Have children write how many on each line.

Direct children to look at the next row of pictures. Read the directions aloud: **Circle which has the greatest number.** Ask: **Which picture should we circle?** the picture of the hamburger Have the children circle the hamburger. Direct the children to look at the next row of pictures. Read the directions aloud: **Circle which has the least number.** Ask: **Which picture should we circle?** the picture of the hot dog Have the children circle the hot dog.

REASONING Say: **Jody says that more people like pizza than hamburgers.** Ask: **Do you agree?** Possible answer: I do not agree. The picture graph shows 5 smiley faces for pizza and 8 for hamburgers. More people like hamburgers.

When counting an item in a picture graph, some children may have trouble tracking from left to right accurately and counting each item. To correct this, have children work with partners and count the items together as they point to each one.

Do the Math page IN68 Read and discuss the fruit picture graph with children. Instruct the children to look at the first row of the graph. Ask: **How many apple pictures are in the first row?** 4 Say: **If there are 4 apple pictures in the row, then 4 children like apples best.**

Assign Exercises 1–3 and monitor children's work.

For Problem 4, have children count the pears and bananas and complete the number sentence.

Children who make more than 1 error in Exercises 1–4 may benefit from the **Alternative Teaching Strategy**.

Alternative Teaching Strategy
On the board, draw a three-row graph labeled *Banana, Apple,* and *Orange.* Draw a different number of smiley faces in each row.

Ask how many children like each kind of fruit and which fruit the most (fewest) children like.

Learn the Math

Use the picture graph.

Food We Like								
🌭	☺	☺	☺					
🍔	☺	☺	☺	☺	☺	☺	☺	☺
🍕	☺	☺	☺	☺	☺			

Write how many.

🌭 _3_   🍔 _8_   🍕 _5_

Circle which has the greatest number.

🌭   (🍔)   🍕

Circle which has the least number.

(🌭)   🍔   🍕

Do the Math

Use the picture graph.

Fruit We Like							
🍎	☺	☺	☺	☺			
🍐	☺	☺	☺	☺	☺	☺	☺
🍌	☺	☺	☺	☺	☺	☺	

Remember
- Read the graph carefully.
- Count how many of each item.

1. Write how many.

🍎 _4_   🍐 _7_   🍌 _6_

2. Circle which has the least number.

(🍎)   🍐   🍌

3. Circle which has the greatest number.

🍎   (🍐)   🍌

4. How many 🍐 and 🍌 in all?

_7_ + _6_ = _13_

Learn the Math

Use the picture graph.

Food We Like								
🌭	☺	☺	☺					
🍔	☺	☺	☺	☺	☺	☺	☺	☺
🍕	☺	☺	☺	☺	☺			

Write how many.

_3_   _____   _____

Circle which has the greatest number.

Circle which has the least number.

Use the picture graph.

Fruit We Like									
🍎	☺	☺	☺	☺					
🍐	☺	☺	☺	☺	☺	☺	☺		
🍌	☺	☺	☺	☺	☺	☺			

1. Write how many.

_____   _____   _____

2. Circle which has the least number.

3. Circle which has the greatest number.

4. How many 🍐 and 🍌 in all?

_____   +   _____   =   _____

Objective
To identify three-dimensional shapes

Vocabulary
sphere A round three-dimensional shape such as a ball

cube A three-dimensional shape with six square faces

cylinder A three-dimensional shape with two circular parallel bases and a curved surface

Manipulatives and Materials
three-dimensional shapes, crayons

COMMON ERROR

- Children may confuse a sphere and a cylinder.

- To correct this, remind children that a sphere is shaped like a basketball and a cylinder is shaped like a can of soup.

Learn the Math page IN71 Show children the three-dimensional shapes of a sphere, a cube, and a cylinder. Ask them to describe each shape in their own words. Guide children through each of the three examples. Encourage them to give some examples of other spheres, cubes, and cylinders found in the classroom or at home.

Guide children through Exercises 1–2. Check that they identify and color the correct shapes.

REASONING Say: Suppose Mia helped her father shop. She found an orange, a can of soup, and a box of cereal. Which object is shaped like a cylinder? the can of soup

Do the Math page IN72 Read and discuss Exercise 1 with children. Remind them to compare the objects to the cylinder and then color the objects that are shaped like the cylinder.

Assign Exercises 2–4 and monitor children's work.

For Problem 5, have children find an example of a sphere in the classroom before beginning to draw. Invite volunteers to describe and name the object they drew.

Children who make more than 1 error in Exercises 1–5 may benefit from the **Alternative Teaching Strategy**.

Alternative Teaching Strategy
Manipulatives and Materials: three-dimensional shapes for a sphere, a cube, and a cylinder; classroom objects shaped like a sphere, a cube, and a cylinder; paper bag

Place classroom objects in a paper bag. Invite a volunteer to choose one object from the bag. Ask that volunteer to describe and identify the kind of three-dimensional shape it may be without looking at it. Then have him or her reveal the object and describe how it compares to the three-dimensional shape.

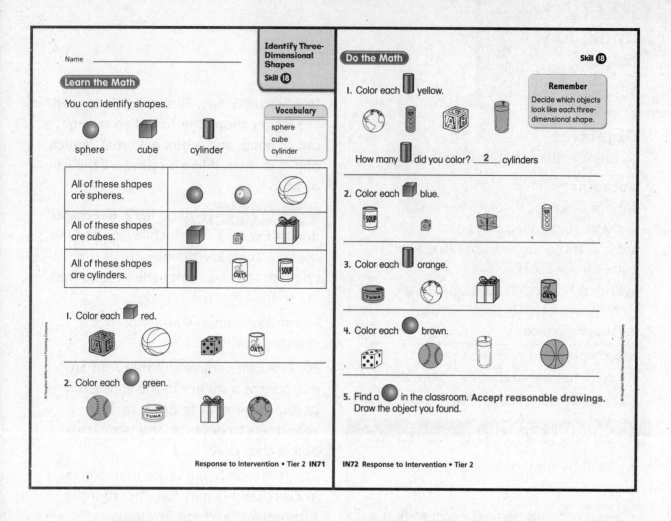

Name _____

Learn the Math

You can identify shapes.

sphere   cube   cylinder

Vocabulary
sphere
cube
cylinder

All of these shapes are spheres.			
All of these shapes are cubes.			
All of these shapes are cylinders.			

1. Color each cube red.

2. Color each sphere green.

Do the Math

1. Color each cylinder yellow.

How many cylinders did you color? __2__ cylinders

Remember
Decide which objects look like each three-dimensional shape.

2. Color each cube blue.

3. Color each cylinder orange.

4. Color each sphere brown.

5. Find a sphere in the classroom. **Accept reasonable drawings.**
Draw the object you found.

Name _____

Learn the Math

You can identify shapes.

 sphere

 cube

 cylinder

All of these shapes are spheres.			
All of these shapes are cubes.			
All of these shapes are cylinders.			

1. Color each red.

2. Color each green.

1. Color each  yellow.

How many did you color? _____ cylinders

2. Color each blue.

3. Color each orange.

4. Color each brown.

5. Find a ⬤ in the classroom. Draw the object you found.

Objective
To identify two-dimensional shapes

Vocabulary
circle A plane curve equidistant from the center

triangle A two-dimensional shape with three sides and three angles

rectangle A two-dimensional shape with four sides and four square corners

square A rectangle with all four sides of equal length

Manipulatives and Materials
two-dimensional (plane) shapes, crayons (see *Teacher Resources*)

COMMON ERROR

- Children may confuse rectangles and squares.

- To correct this, explain that all squares are rectangles. Show them that a square is a special kind of rectangle. It is different from other rectangles because every side of a square is the same length. Show children various examples of squares and rectangles to illustrate the difference in the two types of shapes.

Learn the Math page IN75 Discuss the shapes at the top of the page with children. Ask them to describe each shape in his or her own words. Then guide them through the first example in the table. Ask: **How can you tell if all of the shapes are circles?** Possible answer: all of the shapes are round. Use similar questions for the other shapes in the table. Point out to children that a square is a special kind of rectangle.

Encourage children to use their own descriptions to strengthen understanding of two-dimensional shapes.

REASONING Say: **Suppose Rory says that the classroom door is in the shape of a circle.** Ask: **Do you agree?** No; possible answer: the classroom door is in the shape of a rectangle.

Do the Math page IN76 Read and discuss Exercise 1 with children. Guide them to solve the problem. Ask: **How did you know which shapes were rectangles?** Possible answer: a rectangle has 4 sides and 4 square corners.

Assign Exercises 2–3 and monitor children's work.

Invite children to model Problem 4 with two-dimensional shapes before beginning to draw. Children may wish to trace the model.

Children who make more than 1 error in Exercises 1–4 may benefit from the **Alternative Teaching Strategy**.

Alternative Teaching Strategy
Manipulatives and Materials: two-dimensional (plane) shapes, paper, scissors (see *Teacher Resources*)

Have partners trace and cut out two-dimensional shapes of different types and sizes. Have one partner ask a question such as, **Which is a square?** Have the other partner identify the shape. Have partners repeat the activity with other shapes. Encourage partners to take turns with questions and answers.

© Houghton Mifflin Harcourt Publishing Company

Name _____

Learn the Math

You can identify shapes.

circle   triangle   rectangle   square

Vocabulary

circle
triangle
rectangle
square

All of these shapes are circles.	
All of these shapes are triangles.	
All of these shapes are rectangles.	
All of these shapes are squares.	

1. Color each triangle red.

R

Do the Math

1. Color each rectangle blue.

B   B   B

• Color the rectangles.

• How many rectangles are there? ___3___ .

Remember
A square is a special kind of rectangle.

2. Color each square red.

R   R   R

3. Color each circle green.

G   G   G

4. Draw a house. Use at least 1 rectangle, 1 circle, 1 triangle, and 1 square.

Check children's work.

© Houghton Mifflin Harcourt Publishing Company

Name _____

Learn the Math

You can identify shapes.

circle   triangle   rectangle   square

All of these shapes are circles.	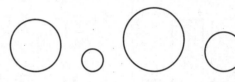
All of these shapes are triangles.	
All of these shapes are rectangles.	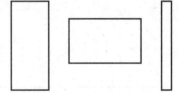
All of these shapes are squares.	

1. Color each triangle red.

1. Color each rectangle blue.

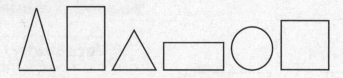

Remember

A square is a special kind of rectangle.

   · Color the rectangles.

   · How many rectangles are there? _____

2. Color each square red.

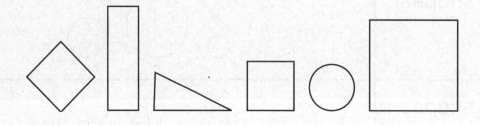

3. Color each circle green.

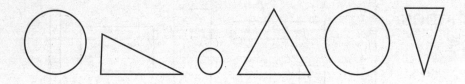

4. Draw a house. Use at least 1 rectangle, 1 circle, 1 triangle, and 1 square.

Count by Tens
Skill 20

Objective
To count by tens on a hundred chart

Materials
hundred chart (see *Teacher Resources*)

COMMON ERROR

- Children may count by tens correctly, but write the incorrect number.

- To correct this, give children a separate hundred chart for each problem. Have them shade the numbers on the hundred chart and then record the numbers.

Learn the Math page IN79 Guide children through the examples. Have them look at Example 1. Ask: **What number do you start on?** Start on 10. **How do you count by tens starting on 10?** 10, 20, 30, 40, 50, 60, 70, 80, 90, 100 **What pattern do you see?** Possible answers: the numbers have a 0 in the ones place; the numbers in the tens place increase by 1 ten for each row.

Have children look at Example 2. Ask: **What number do you start on?** Start on 4. **How do you count by tens starting on 4?** 4, 14, 24, 34, 44, 54, 64, 74, 84, 94 **What pattern do you see?** Possible answers: the numbers have a 4 in the ones place; the numbers in the tens place increase by 1 ten for each row.

REASONING Say: Explain how to use a hundred chart to count by tens starting on 6. Possible answer: I start on 6 and count by 1 ten. It is 16. Then I count by 1 more ten from 16. It is 26. I do this until I reach the end which is 96.

Do the Math page IN80 Read and discuss Exercise 1 with children. Ask: **How do you count by tens starting on 5?** Possible answer: I look at 5 on the hundred chart. Then I look at the numbers down that column: 5, 15, 25, 35, 45, 55, 65, 75, 85, 95.

Assign Exercises 2–4 and monitor children's work.

Encourage children to use the hundred chart to solve Problem 5. Have them write the numbers in the tens pattern to find the number on which Mike stopped, 93.

Children who make more than 1 error in Exercises 1–5 may benefit from the **Alternative Teaching Strategy**.

Alternative Teaching Strategy
Materials: hundred chart (see *Teacher Resources*)

Write a problem for counting by tens on the board. Include the start number, as well as the stop number, on the hundred chart. Demonstrate for children on the hundred chart how to shade the start number, the stop number, as well as the numbers in between. Then invite a volunteer to count by tens orally. To repeat the activity, have children shade the tens pattern with a different color for each problem.

Learn the Math

You can count by tens on a hundred chart.

Example 1

Start on 10.
Count by tens.
Write the numbers.

1	2	3	4	5	6	7	8	9	10
11	12	13	14	15	16	17	18	19	20
21	22	23	24	25	26	27	28	29	30
31	32	33	34	35	36	37	38	39	40
41	42	43	44	45	46	47	48	49	50
51	52	53	54	55	56	57	58	59	60
61	62	63	64	65	66	67	68	69	70
71	72	73	74	75	76	77	78	79	80
81	82	83	84	85	86	87	88	89	90
91	92	93	94	95	96	97	98	99	100

10, 20, __30__, 40, __50__, __60__, __70__, 80, __90__, 100

Example 2

Start on 4.
Count by tens.
Write the numbers.

1	2	3	4	5	6	7	8	9	10
11	12	13	14	15	16	17	18	19	20
21	22	23	24	25	26	27	28	29	30
31	32	33	34	35	36	37	38	39	40
41	42	43	44	45	46	47	48	49	50
51	52	53	54	55	56	57	58	59	60
61	62	63	64	65	66	67	68	69	70
71	72	73	74	75	76	77	78	79	80
81	82	83	84	85	86	87	88	89	90
91	92	93	94	95	96	97	98	99	100

4, 14, 24, __34__, __44__, 54, __64__, 74, 84, __94__

Count by tens. Write the numbers.

Remember
Each row is a group of 10 squares.

1. Start on 5.

   • On what number will you start? __5__

   • What will the next number be? __15__

   • Is this number 10 more than 5? __Yes__

   • On what number will you stop the count? __95__

1	2	3	4	5	6	7	8	9	10
11	12	13	14	15	16	17	18	19	20
21	22	23	24	25	26	27	28	29	30
31	32	33	34	35	36	37	38	39	40
41	42	43	44	45	46	47	48	49	50
51	52	53	54	55	56	57	58	59	60
61	62	63	64	65	66	67	68	69	70
71	72	73	74	75	76	77	78	79	80
81	82	83	84	85	86	87	88	89	90
91	92	93	94	95	96	97	98	99	100

   • Write the numbers.

   5, 15, __25__, __35__, __45__, 55, __65__, __75__, __85__, __95__

2. Start on 7.

   7, 17, __27__, __37__, __47__, __57__, __67__, __77__, __87__, __97__

3. Start on 2.

   2, 12, __22__, __32__, __42__, __52__, __62__, __72__, __82__, __92__

4. Start on 9.

   9, 19, __29__, __39__, __49__, __59__, __69__, __79__, __89__, __99__

5. Mike counted by tens on a hundred chart.
   He started on 3. On what number did he stop the count?

   3, 13, __23__, __33__, __43__, __53__, __63__, __73__, __83__, __93__

   Mike stopped the count on __93__.

Name _____

Learn the Math

You can count by tens on a hundred chart.

Example 1

Start on 10.
Count by tens.
Write the numbers.

1	2	3	4	5	6	7	8	9	10
11	12	13	14	15	16	17	18	19	20
21	22	23	24	25	26	27	28	29	30
31	32	33	34	35	36	37	38	39	40
41	42	43	44	45	46	47	48	49	50
51	52	53	54	55	56	57	58	59	60
61	62	63	64	65	66	67	68	69	70
71	72	73	74	75	76	77	78	79	80
81	82	83	84	85	86	87	88	89	90
91	92	93	94	95	96	97	98	99	100

10, 20, _____, 40, _____, _____, _____, 80, _____, 100

Example 2

Start on 4.
Count by tens.
Write the numbers.

1	2	3	4	5	6	7	8	9	10
11	12	13	14	15	16	17	18	19	20
21	22	23	24	25	26	27	28	29	30
31	32	33	34	35	36	37	38	39	40
41	42	43	44	45	46	47	48	49	50
51	52	53	54	55	56	57	58	59	60
61	62	63	64	65	66	67	68	69	70
71	72	73	74	75	76	77	78	79	80
81	82	83	84	85	86	87	88	89	90
91	92	93	94	95	96	97	98	99	100

4, 14, 24, _____, _____, 54, _____, 74, 84, _____

Count by tens. Write the numbers.

1. Start on 5.

- On what number will you start? _____

- What will the next number be? _____

- Is this number 10 more than 5? _____

- On what number will you stop the count? _____

- Write the numbers.

1	2	3	4	5	6	7	8	9	10
11	12	13	14	15	16	17	18	19	20
21	22	23	24	25	26	27	28	29	30
31	32	33	34	35	36	37	38	39	40
41	42	43	44	45	46	47	48	49	50
51	52	53	54	55	56	57	58	59	60
61	62	63	64	65	66	67	68	69	70
71	72	73	74	75	76	77	78	79	80
81	82	83	84	85	86	87	88	89	90
91	92	93	94	95	96	97	98	99	100

5, 15, _____, _____, _____, _____, _____, _____, _____, _____

2. Start on 7.

7, 17, _____, _____, _____, _____, _____, _____, _____, _____

3. Start on 2.

2, 12, _____, _____, _____, _____, _____, _____, _____, _____

4. Start on 9.

9, 19, _____, _____, _____, _____, _____, _____, _____, _____

5. Mike counted by tens on a hundred chart.
He started on 3. On what number did he stop the count?

3, 13, _____, _____, _____, _____, _____, _____, _____, _____

Mike stopped the count on _____.

Identify Patterns
Skill 21

Objective
To identify repeating patterns

Materials
two-dimensional shapes (see *Teacher Resources*)

COMMON ERROR

- Children may find it difficult to identify the pattern being used.

- To correct this, show children how to identify the pattern unit before it begins to repeat.

Learn the Math page IN83 Look at the pattern in Step 1 with children. Ask a volunteer to describe the colors in the pattern. Ask: **What do you notice about the colors?** Possible answer: The colors are gray, black, and white. The colors repeat.

For Step 2, show children how to find the pattern unit that repeats. Help them say the pattern aloud, then go back and identify the pattern unit before the repeat begins. Then ask them to trace the ring.

For Step 3, discuss how the first shapes in the pattern have been colored. gray, black, white, gray Ask: **What color will the next shape in the pattern be? Explain how you know.** Possible answer: Black; the pattern unit is gray, black, white. So black will be the next color after gray.

Work through Exercises 1–2 with children. For Exercise 2, guide them to see that the part of the pattern that repeats is black, gray, gray.

REASONING Ask: **How can you check to see if a pattern is continued correctly?** Possible answer: I can find the part of the pattern that repeats over and over and then use that part to continue the pattern.

Do the Math page IN84 Read and discuss Exercise 1 with children. Guide them to solve the problem. Ask: **What two colors are in the pattern?** gray, black **What is the pattern unit?** gray square, black square

Assign Exercises 2–4 and monitor children's work. Check that children are using the part of the pattern that repeats to continue the pattern.

For Problem 5, encourage children to use two-dimensional shapes to make a model of the pattern. Have them leave a space in the pattern and then decide which shape is missing (a black circle).

Children who make more than 1 error in Exercises 1–5 may benefit from the **Alternative Teaching Strategy.**

Alternative Teaching Strategy
Manipulatives: connecting cubes

Model for children an AB pattern with a connecting cube train in which the pattern repeats four times. Have partners copy the model with their own connecting cubes. Then have them separate the first two cubes from the cube train. Partners work together as they place the two cubes along the cube train to see how the pattern repeats over and over. Extend the activity to include ABB and ABC patterns.

© Houghton Mifflin Harcourt Publishing Company

Learn the Math

You can find a pattern.

Step 1 Read the pattern.	● ● ○ ● ● ○
Step 2 Find the pattern unit. Identify the pattern.	● ● ○ ● ● ○
Step 3 Color the shapes to continue the pattern.	● ● ○ ● ○ ○ ○ ○ black, white, gray, black

Find the pattern. Then color to continue it.

1. ■ ■ ■ ■ ■ ■ □ □
   gray, black

2. ▲ ▲ ▲ ▲ ▲ ▲ ▲ △ △
   gray, gray

Response to Intervention • Tier 2 **IN83**

Do the Math

Skill 21

Find the pattern unit. Color to continue it.

1. ■ ■ ■ ■ ■ ■ □ □
   gray, black

   · What two colors are in the pattern?
     gray, black

   · What is the pattern unit?
     gray square, black square

2. ● ● ● ● ● ● ○ ○
   black, gray

3. ▲ △ ▲ △ ▲ ▲ △ △
   white, black

4. 🐻 🐻 🐻 🐻 🐻 🐻 🐻 🐻
   black, gray

5. Which shape is missing?
   Draw and color the shape.

   ■ ● ● ■ ○ ● ■ ●
   black

IN84 Response to Intervention • Tier 2

Learn the Math

You can find a pattern.

Step 1 Read the pattern.	🔵 ⚫ ⚪ 🔵 ⚫ ⚪
Step 2 Find the pattern unit. Identify the pattern.	(🔵 ⚫ ⚪) 🔵 ⚫ ⚪
Step 3 Color the shapes to continue the pattern.	🔵 ⚫ ⚪ 🔵 ⚪ ⚪ ⚪ ⚪

Find the pattern. Then color to continue it.

1.

2. ▲ ▲ ▲ ▲ ▲ ▲ ▲ △ △

Find the pattern unit. Color to continue it.

1. ▣ ■ ▣ ■ ▣ ■ ☐ ☐

- What two colors are in the pattern?

_____

- What is the pattern unit?

_____

2. ● ● ● ● ● ● ○ ○

3. ▲ △ ▲ ▲ △ ▲ ▲ △ △

4. 🐻 🐻 🐻 🐻 🐻 🐻 🐻 🐻

5. Which shape is missing?
   Draw and color the shape.

Objective
To compare lengths of objects

Vocabulary
longer Having greater length than another

shorter Having less length than another

Manipulatives
connecting cubes

COMMON ERROR

- Children may have difficulty comparing lengths.

- To correct this, have children use a train of connecting cubes about the same length as the objects they are comparing. Children can count the number of cubes to compare.

Learn the Math page IN87 Have children use connecting cube trains to represent the pictures in the model. Have them align the two cube trains on the left side to compare. Ask children to identify the train that is longer. Then ask them to identify the train that is shorter.

Guide children through Exercises 1–4. Encourage children to model the pictures with cube trains.

REASONING Say: **Suppose Doug says that a paper clip is longer than a baseball bat.** Ask: **Is he correct? Explain.** No; possible answer: a paper clip is shorter than a baseball bat.

Do the Math page IN88 Read the directions with children. Work through the first exercise together. Ask: **Which object is longer? Circle it.** Check that children circle the longer object. Ask: **Which object is shorter? Draw a line under it.** Check that children underline the shorter object.

Assign Exercises 2–5 and monitor children's work.

For Problem 6, have children use connecting cubes to build a cube train that is longer than the crayon. Then have them trace their cube train in the answer space below the crayon. Guide children to start the drawing on the left side to show the comparison.

Children who make more than 1 error in Exercises 1–6 may benefit from the **Alternative Teaching Strategy.**

Alternative Teaching Strategy
Materials: ribbon or string lengths, paper, crayons

Have children use a length of ribbon to model shorter and longer lengths. Give each child a length of ribbon. Have them find an object in the classroom that is shorter than their length of ribbon. Then have them find an object that is longer than their length of ribbon. Invite children to draw their results.

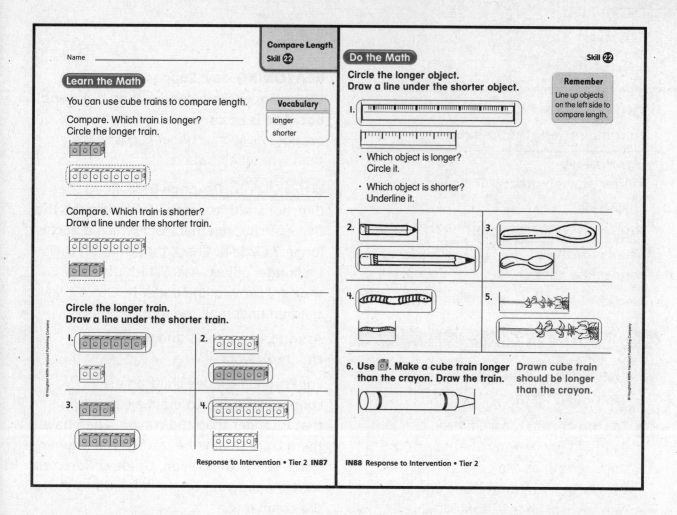

Learn the Math

You can use cube trains to compare length.

Compare. Which train is longer?
Circle the longer train.

Vocabulary
longer
shorter

Compare. Which train is shorter?
Draw a line under the shorter train.

Circle the longer train.
Draw a line under the shorter train.

1.

2.

3.

4.

Do the Math

Circle the longer object.
Draw a line under the shorter object.

Remember
Line up objects
on the left side to
compare length.

1.

- Which object is longer?
  Circle it.

- Which object is shorter?
  Underline it.

2.

3.

4.

5.

6. Use 🎲. Make a cube train longer than the crayon. Draw the train.

Drawn cube train should be longer than the crayon.

Name _____

Learn the Math

You can use cube trains to compare length.

Compare. Which train is longer?
Circle the longer train.

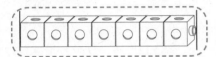

Compare. Which train is shorter?
Draw a line under the shorter train.

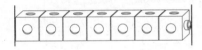

Circle the longer train.
Draw a line under the shorter train.

I.

2.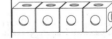

3.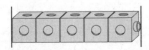

4.

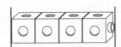

Circle the longer object.
Draw a line under the shorter object.

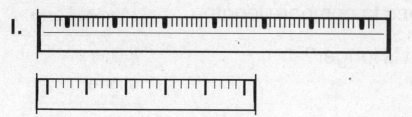

I.

- Which object is longer?
  Circle it.

- Which object is shorter?
  Underline it.

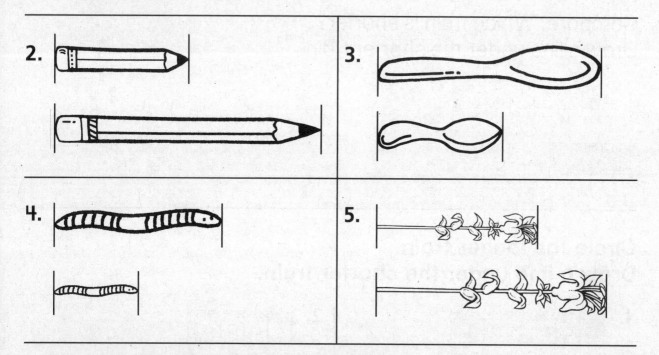

2.

3.

4.

5.

6. Use . Make a cube train longer than the crayon. Draw the train.

Objective
To compare objects by weight

Vocabulary
lighter Having less weight than another

heavier Having more weight than another

Materials
classroom objects

COMMON ERROR

- Children may not understand the meanings of the words "heavier" and "lighter" when comparing the weights of objects.

- To correct this, give children plenty of examples of objects that are heavy and objects that are light, and model how you compare those objects. Stress the use of the terms "heavier" and "lighter" when you talk about the objects.

Learn the Math page IN91 Discuss the objects shown at the top of the page. Guide children through Step 1. Demonstrate how to pick up one object in each hand and compare the weights of the objects. Ask: **Does the water bottle feel lighter than the pencil?** no

Guide children through Step 2. Ask: **Does the book feel lighter than the pencil?** no

For Step 3, guide children to compare the paper clip and the pencil. Ask: **Does the paper clip feel lighter than the pencil?** yes

REASONING Say: Suppose Eric says that a grape feels heavier than a watermelon. Ask: **Is he correct? Explain.** No; possible answer: I can hold a grape in one hand, but I need both hands to hold a watermelon. So, a grape feels lighter than a watermelon.

Do the Math page IN92 Read and discuss Exercise 1 with children. Guide them to solve the problem. Ask: **How did you decide which object feels heavier than the scissors?** Possible answer: I held them in my hands to compare.

Assign Exercises 2–7 and monitor children's work.

Have children read Problem 8 and then decide which picture shows the lighter object. Children may want to use classroom objects to compare the weights.

Children who make more than 2 errors in Exercises 1–8 may benefit from the **Alternative Teaching Strategy**.

Alternative Teaching Strategy
Materials: classroom objects, paper

Have children compare weights of objects having extreme differences in weight, rather than objects that are only slightly different in weight. For example, give children an eraser and a dictionary. Invite children to hold one object at a time to fully explore the weight of the object. Then have them hold one object in each hand to compare the weights of the objects. Encourage them to record and complete the statement: The ____ feels heavier/lighter than the ____.

Name _____

Learn the Math

You can hold objects to compare
the weights.

Which object feels lighter than the pencil?

Step 1 Hold one object in each hand. Compare.	The ⬜ feels heavier than the ✏.
Step 2 Try another object. Compare.	The 📕 feels heavier than the ✏.
Step 3 Try another object. Compare.	The ▭ feels lighter than the ✏.

So, the ▭ feels lighter than the ✏ .

**Hold one object in each hand. Circle the
picture of the object that feels heavier.**

1. ✏ | ⚾   2. 🪙 | 🧮

Do the Math

1. Which object feels heavier than the scissors?

- Is the ▭ heavier than the ✂ ? __no__
- Is the 🎒 heavier than the ✂ ? __yes__
- Circle the object that feels heavier.

**Hold one object in each hand. Circle the
picture of the object that feels heavier.**

2. ✏ | 📓   3. 📱 | 🧵

4. ➰ | ⬛   5. Glue | 🖌

6. 👟 | ERASER   7. 📏 | 🗜

8. Kim had these two objects. She put the
lighter object on the table. Circle the
object she put on the table.

Name _____

Learn the Math

You can hold objects to compare the weights.

Which object feels lighter than the pencil?

Vocabulary

lighter
heavier

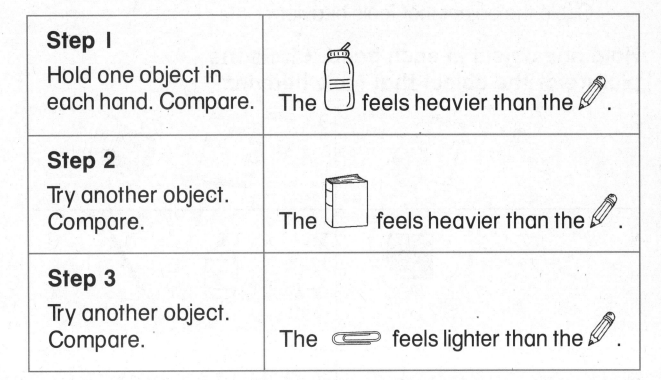

Step 1 Hold one object in each hand. Compare.	The ☐ feels heavier than the ✏.
Step 2 Try another object. Compare.	The ☐ feels heavier than the ✏.
Step 3 Try another object. Compare.	The ⌗ feels lighter than the ✏.

So, the _____ feels lighter than the ✏.

Hold one object in each hand. Circle the picture of the object that feels heavier.

1.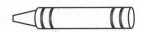

2.

1. Which object feels heavier than the scissors?

 |

- Is the heavier than the ? _____

- Is the heavier than the ? _____

- Circle the object that feels heavier.

Hold one object in each hand. Circle the picture of the object that feels heavier.

2.

3.

4.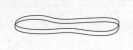

5.

6.

7.

8. Kim had these two objects. She put the lighter object on the table. Circle the object she put on the table.

Use a Number Line
Skill 24

Objective
To use a number line to determine before and after

Vocabulary
before In front of a given number
after Following a given number

COMMON ERROR

- Children may get confused about before and after.
- To correct this, review the terms using objects so children can visualize the meaning of each term.

Learn the Math page IN95 Read and discuss the example with children. Use the number line to explain to children the meanings of *just before* and *just after*. Ask: **What do you notice about the position of the numbers that are *just before?*** Possible answer: they are to the left of the given number. Work through Exercises 1–5 with children. Ask: **How do you know if you are looking for the number that is *just before* or *just after?*** Possible answer: I look for the empty box.

REASONING Ask: **Lana says that 43 is between 44 and 46. Do you agree?** No; possible answer: if I look on a number line, I see that 43 is between 42 and 44. Use a number line to demonstrate how to find the answer.

Do the Math page IN96 Read and discuss Exercise 1 with children. Guide children to solve the problem.

Ask: **How does the number line help you find the missing number?** Possible answer: the number line helps me count forward or count back to find the missing number.

Assign Exercises 2–7 and monitor children's work.

For Problem 8, ask: **How did you know the order in which to write the names?** Jackie was between Shanna and Emilio. Since Emilio was just after Jackie, I knew Shanna was just before Jackie. Discuss the question with children.

Children who make more than 2 errors in Exercises 1–8 may benefit from the **Alternative Teaching Strategy**.

Alternative Teaching Strategy
Materials: masking tape, index cards

On the floor, make a number line from 1 to 12 using masking tape and numbered index cards.

Have partners take turns turning over one of the index cards. The other partner should say the hidden number. Children can turn the index card over to check.

Ask: **What number is hidden? What number is before (after) the hidden number? The hidden number is between which two numbers?**

Learn the Math

You can use a number line to find the number that is just before or just after other numbers.

Vocabulary
before
after

1 2 3 4 **5** 6 **7** 8 9 10 11 12

5 is just before 6.

7 is just after 6.

Write the number that is just before or just after.

1. **10** 11 12

2. 9 10 **11**

3. 32 33 **34**

4. **55** 56 57

5. **49** 50 51

Do the Math

Write the number that is just before or just after.

1. **87** 88 89

- Do you need to find the number that is just before or just after?
  just before

- What number is just before 88?
  87

So, **87** is just before 88.

Remember
Use the number line to help you decide if you need to find the number just before or just after.

2. 7 8 **9**

3. **58** 59 60

4. **44** 45 46

5. 90 91 **92**

6. **35** 36 37

7. 25 26 **27**

Use the clues. Write the names in order.

8. Jackie, Shanna, and Emilio are in line.
Jackie is between Shanna and Emilio.
Emilio is just after Jackie.

Shanna **Jackie** **Emilio**

Learn the Math

You can use a number line to find the number that is just before or just after other numbers.

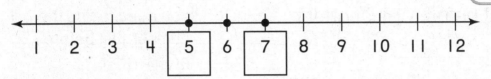

5 is just before 6.

[ ] is just after 6.

Write the number that is just before or just after.

1.

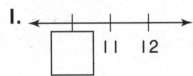

11   12

2.

9   10   [ ]

3.

32   33   [ ]

4.

[ ]   56   57

5.

[ ]   50   51

Do the Math

Write the number that is just before or just after.

1.

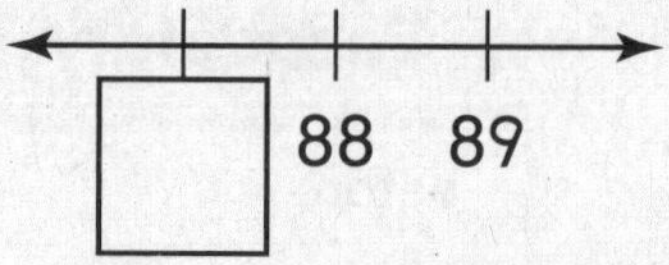

- Do you need to find the number that is just before or just after?

____

- What number is just before 88?

____

So, ________ is just before 88.

Remember

Use the number line to help you decide if you need to find the number just before or just after.

2.

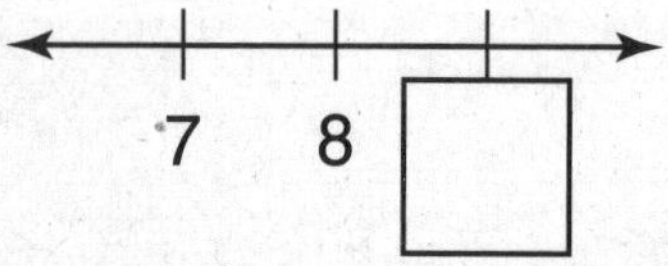

3.

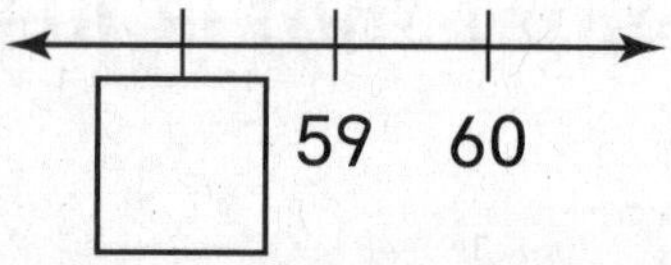

4.

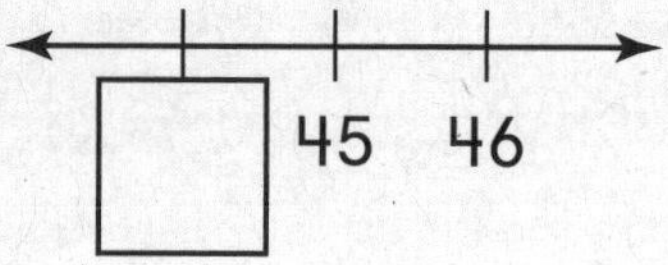

5.

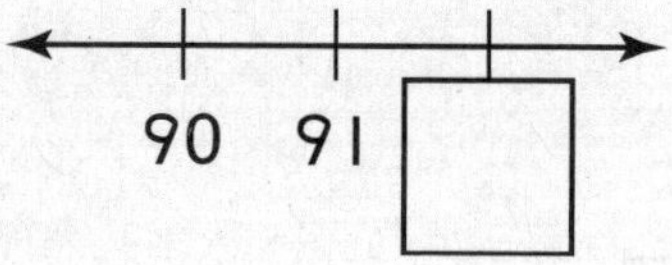

6.

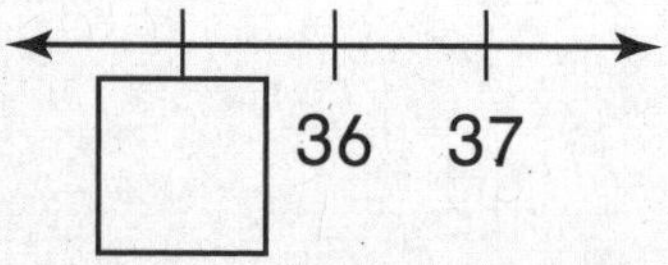

7.

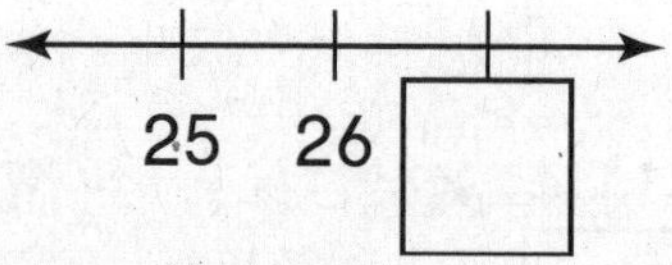

Use the clues. Write the names in order.

8. Jackie, Shanna, and Emilio are in line.
Jackie is between Shanna and Emilio.
Emilio is just after Jackie.

______________ ______________ ______________

Skip Count by Fives and Tens

Skill 25

Objective
To skip count by fives and tens using pictures

COMMON ERROR

- Children may miss a number as they are skip counting.

- To correct this, have children use a hundred chart to check their work. Children can count by fives or tens and circle each number. They can then count the circled numbers aloud.

Learn the Math page IN99 Read and discuss the first problem with children. Ask: **How are the groups of seeds you are counting alike?** Each group has the same number of seeds, 5. Have children count the seeds in each apple to check that each one has five seeds. Ask: **What number will you say first when skip counting by fives?** 5 Skip count aloud as a class to complete the problem. Ask: **What pattern do you see?** Possible answer: the digits in the ones place are 5, 0, 5, 0.

In the second problem, the pattern is different. Ask: **What pattern do you see when counting by tens?** The digit in the ones place is always 0. **How many toes are there in all?** 80

REASONING Say: **Jeff was counting by tens. He counted 5, 10, 20, 25, and 30.** Ask: **Did he count correctly?** no

Do the Math page IN100 Read and discuss Exercise 1 with children. Guide children to solve the problem. Ask: **Do all of the groups have the same number of oranges?** yes Discuss with children why this means they can skip count to find the total number of oranges. Ask: **What number do you skip count the oranges by?** fives

Assign Exercises 2–3 and monitor children's work.

For Problems 4 and 5, encourage children to draw a picture or use counters to help them count.

Children who make more than 1 error in Exercises 1–5 may benefit from the **Alternative Teaching Strategy**.

Alternative Teaching Strategy
Materials: 100 connecting cubes

Help children connect the cubes in trains of ten. Count by tens to find out how many there are in all.

Break each of the trains into two trains of five cubes each. Count by fives to 100. Have children explain how they can keep track of the trains they have already counted. Ask: **Why do you get the same number when you count by fives as you do when you count by tens?** Possible answer: they are the same cubes. I just counted in a different way.

Name _____

Learn the Math

You can use a picture to skip count by fives and tens.

Skip count. Count the seeds by fives.
Write how many.

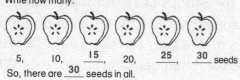

5, 10, 15, 20, 25, 30 seeds

So, there are __30__ seeds in all.

Skip count. Count the toes by tens.
Write how many.

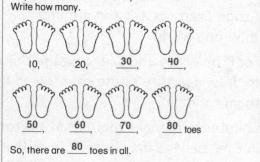

10, 20, 30, 40,

50, 60, 70, 80 toes

So, there are __80__ toes in all.

Skip count. Write how many.

1.

    5, 10, 15, 20, 25, 30 oranges

    · How many oranges are in each group? __5__

    · When you count by fives, what is the first number? __5__

    So, there are __30__ oranges.

> **Remember**
> · Read the problem carefully before skip counting.
> · When you count by fives, the digit in the ones place will be a 0 or a 5.
> · When you count by tens, the digit in the ones place will always be a 0.

2.

    5, 10, 15, 20, 25, 30, 35 strawberries

3.

    10, 20, 30, 40 fingers

---

4. Liam has 5 groups of 10 pennies. How many pennies does he have in all? Count the pennies by tens.

   10, 20, 30, 40, 50;

   50 pennies

5. April has 7 groups of 5 gumdrops. How many gumdrops does she have in all? Count the gumdrops by fives.

   5, 10, 15, 20, 25, 30, 35;

   35 gumdrops

Name _____

Learn the Math

You can use a picture to skip count by fives and tens.

Skip count. Count the seeds by fives.
Write how many.

5,   10,   ____,   20,   ____,   ____ seeds

So, there are ____ seeds in all.

Skip count. Count the toes by tens.
Write how many.

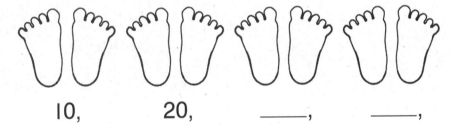

10,   20,   ____,   ____,

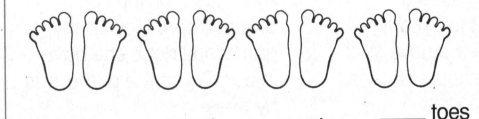

____,   ____,   ____,   ____ toes

So, there are ____ toes in all.

Skip count. Write how many.

1.

——, ——, ——, ——, ——, —— oranges

- How many oranges are in each group? ____

- When you count by fives, what is the first number? ____

So, there are ____ oranges.

2.

——, ——, ——, ——, ——, ——, —— strawberries

3.

——, ——, ——, ____ fingers

_____

4. Liam has 5 groups of 10 pennies. How many pennies does he have in all? Count the pennies by tens.

5. April has 7 groups of 5 gumdrops. How many gumdrops does she have in all? Count the gumdrops by fives.

Make a Model •
Model Addition

Problem Solving Strategy I

Objective
To use the strategy *make a model* to model addition problems

Manipulatives
two-color counters

COMMON ERROR

- Children may not join the two groups to find the total.

- To correct this, give each child a cup in which to drop the two groups of counters as they count how many there are in all.

Problem Solving — page IN102

- **What do I need to find?** Read through the story problem with children. Ask: **What is the problem to solve?** to find out how many frogs there are in the pond in all

- **What information do I need to use?** Have children reread the problem. Ask: **What two pieces of information tell you the numbers to use?** 3 frogs; 2 more frogs

- **Show how to solve the problem.** Have children use two-color counters to solve the problem. Have them use one color counter to represent the frogs in the pond and another color to represent the frogs that join them. Ask: **How many counters do you need for the frogs in the pond?** 3 counters **How many counters do you need for the frogs who joined them?** 2 counters Have children count the total number of counters. Ask: **So, how many frogs are there in all?** 5 frogs Have children draw counters to show how many in all.

Assign Exercises 1–2 and monitor children's work. Encourage children to use counters and then draw to show their work. Have them write how many there are in all.

Children who make more than 1 error in Exercises 1–2 may benefit from the **Alternative Teaching Strategy**.

Alternative Teaching Strategy
Manipulatives: connecting cubes

Have children use connecting cubes to model addition problems. Write an addition story problem on the board. Have children use one color cube to represent one group and another color cube to represent the other group. Have them connect the cubes and tell how many cubes there are in all.

For answer page, see p. IN107.

Name _____

Problem Solving

3 frogs are in the pond.
Then 2 more frogs join them.
How many frogs are there in all?

What do I need to find?	**What information do I need to use?**
Find out how many _____ are in the pond in all.	_____ frogs
	_____ more frogs

Show how to solve the problem.

3   plus   2   _____ in all

Use to solve. Draw the .

I. Lee sees 3 ants. 4 more
ants come. How many ants
are there in all?

_____ ants

_____

2. Jon has 4 worms. He gets
2 more worms. How many
worms does he have in all?

_____ worms

Draw a Picture • Addition Word Problems

Problem Solving Strategy 2

Objective
To use the strategy *draw a picture* to model addition problems

Problem Solving page IN104

• **What do I need to find?** Read through the story problem with children. Ask: **What is the problem to solve?** how many marbles Mia and Kim have in all

• **What information do I need to use?** Have children reread the problem. Ask: **What two pieces of information tell you the numbers to use?** Mia has 9 marbles; Kim has 2 fewer marbles than Mia.

• **Show how to solve the problem.** Have children draw a diagram to solve the problem. Have them draw a group

of simple shapes or marks to show the number of marbles Mia has, as well as a group to show how many marbles Kim has. Ask: **How many marks do you need for Mia's marbles?** 9 marks **How many marks do you need for Kim's marbles?** 7 marks Have children count the total number of marks. Ask: **How many marbles do Mia and Kim have in all?** 16 marbles Have them draw and label their diagrams to show how many in all.

Assign Exercises 1–2 and monitor children's work. Guide children to draw diagrams to show their work. Have them write how many there are in all.

Children who make more than 1 error in Exercises 1–2 may benefit from the **Alternative Teaching Strategy**.

Alternative Teaching Strategy
Manipulatives and Materials: two-color counters, crayons

Have children use two-color counters to model the addends in an addition word problem. Encourage them to use a different color counter to model each addend. Then have them draw a diagram to represent the counters they used to solve the problem. Invite volunteers to tell how their diagrams show the answer to the problem.

For answer page, see p. IN107.

Name _____

Problem Solving

Mia has 9 marbles. Kim has 2 fewer
marbles than Mia. How many marbles
do they have in all?

What do I need to find?	**What information do I need to use?**
Find how many _____ they have in all.	Mia has ____ marbles. Kim has ____ fewer marbles.

Show how to solve the problem.

_____ marbles in all

Draw a picture to solve.

1. Roy has 6 pens. Tim has 2 more
pens than Roy. How many pens do
they have in all?

_____ pens

2. Kate has 7 rocks. Todd has 3 fewer
rocks than Kate. How many rocks do
they have in all?

_____ rocks

Act It Out • Subtraction Word Problems

Problem Solving Strategy 3

Objective
To use the strategy *act it out* to model subtraction problems

Manipulatives
counters

COMMON ERROR

- Children may remove the wrong number of counters when acting out subtraction problems.

- To correct this, have children arrange counters on their desks. As they remove each counter, have them place it to the side. Then have them count the remaining counters.

Problem Solving page IN106

- **What do I need to find?** Read through the story problem with children. Ask: **What is the problem to solve?** how many books Cindy gives to Pam

- **What information do I need to use?** Have children reread the problem. Ask: **What two pieces of information tell you the numbers to use?** Cindy has 11 books; Cindy has 6 books left.

- **Show how to solve the problem.** Have children use counters to solve the problem. Ask: **How many counters do you need for the books Cindy has?** 11 counters **How many of those 11 counters do you need to show the books Cindy has left?** 6 counters Have children remove all but 6 counters. Ask: **How many counters did you take away?** 5 counters **So, how many books does Cindy give to Pam?** 5 books Have children draw 11 counters and circle a group of 6 of those counters. Have them circle and mark an X on the group of 5 counters to show the number of books Cindy gives to Pam.

Assign Exercises 1–2 and monitor children's work. Encourage children to use counters and then draw to show their work. Check that children draw a circle and an X around the group that is subtracted.

Children who make more than 1 error in Exercises 1–2 may benefit from the **Alternative Teaching Strategy**.

Alternative Teaching Strategy
Have volunteers act out a subtraction word problem, such as: **There are 9 children standing in a circle. Then some children sit. If 5 children are left standing in the circle, how many children sit?** Have 9 volunteers supply the action in the problem while the class solves the problem. 4 children sit. Invite new volunteers to act out similar problems.

For answer page, see p. IN107.

Problem Solving

Cindy has 11 books. She gives some to Pam. She has 6 left. How many books does she give to Pam?

What do I need to find?	**What information do I need to use?**
Find how many _____ Cindy gives to Pam.	Cindy has _____ books. Cindy has _____ books left.

Show how to solve the problem.

Cindy gives Pam _____ books.

Act it out to solve.
Draw to show your work.

1. Rob has 13 cubes. Some are red and some are blue. He has 5 blue cubes. How many cubes are red?

_____ red cubes

2. Ben has 16 toy cars. He gives some away. He has 9 left. How many toy cars does he give away?

_____ toy cars

Name _____

Problem Solving

3 frogs are in the pond.
Then 2 more frogs join them.
How many frogs are there in all?

What do I need to find?	What information do I need to use?
Find out how many __frogs__ are in the pond in all.	__3__ frogs __2__ more frogs

Show how to solve the problem.

○ ○ ○   ○ ○

3   plus   2   __5__ in all

Use ● to solve. Draw the ●.

I. Lee sees 3 ants. 4 more ants come. How many ants are there in all?

○ ○ ○   ○ ○ ○ ○   __7__ ants

2. Jon has 4 worms. He gets 2 more worms. How many worms does he have in all?

○ ○ ○ ○   ○ ○   __6__ worms

IN102 Response to Intervention • Tier 2

Name _____

Problem Solving

Mia has 9 marbles. Kim has 2 fewer marbles than Mia. How many marbles do they have in all?

What do I need to find?	What information do I need to use?
Find how many __marbles__ they have in all.	Mia has __9__ marbles. Kim has __2__ fewer marbles.

Show how to solve the problem.

9 marbles   X X X X X X X X X
7 marbles   X X X X X X X

__16__ marbles in all

Draw a picture to solve.   Check children's pictures.

I. Roy has 6 pens. Tim has 2 more pens than Roy. How many pens do they have in all?

__14__ pens

2. Kate has 7 rocks. Todd has 3 fewer rocks than Kate. How many rocks do they have in all?

__11__ rocks

IN104 Response to Intervention • Tier 2

Name _____

Problem Solving

Cindy has 11 books. She gives some to Pam. She has 6 left. How many books does she give to Pam?

What do I need to find?	What information do I need to use?
Find how many __books__ Cindy gives to Pam.	Cindy has __11__ books. Cindy has __6__ books left.

Show how to solve the problem.

(○ ○ ○ ○ ○ ○) (⊗ ⊗ ⊗ ⊗ ⊗)

Cindy gives Pam __5__ books.

Act it out to solve.   Check children's drawings.
Draw to show your work.

I. Rob has 13 cubes. Some are red and some are blue. He has 5 blue cubes. How many cubes are red?   __8__ red cubes

2. Ben has 16 toy cars. He gives some away. He has 9 left. How many toy cars does he give away?   __7__ toy cars

IN106 Response to Intervention • Tier 2

Objective
To sort objects by one attribute: size

Materials
classroom objects such as books

COMMON ERROR

- Children may have difficulty recognizing a picture of an object that is a different size from other objects.

- Provide children with sorting experiences with concrete objects. Make a group of two books that are the same size and one book that is larger. Have children find the books that are the same size. Then ask: **Which book is larger?** Have children draw the objects and draw a ring around the larger object. Continue with groups of other classroom objects.

Learn the Math page IN111 Explain that the first row shows a group of tall glasses, and point out that one glass does not belong in the group. Have children point to each glass and say if it is tall or short. Ask: **Which glass does not belong in the group? Why?** The third glass; it is shorter than the others. Have children complete the rest of the exercises on the page. Point out that the objects in the third row are arranged differently than the objects in the first two rows, but children should still find the one that does not belong.

REASONING Display a group of five classroom books. Have three of the books be the same size. Ask: **How can we sort these books?** Make a group of the books that are the same size. Have children explain why the other books do not belong in the group.

Do the Math page IN112 Read the directions. Remind children that each row shows a group of objects. One object does not belong in the group. Help children find the one that does not belong. Ask: **How can you find the one that does not belong in the group?** Look for the one that is longer, taller, shorter, or smaller. Tell children to mark an X on the one that does not belong.

Assign Exercises 2 and 3 and monitor children as they work.

Children who make more than 1 error in Exercises 1–3 may benefit from the **Alternative Teaching Strategy**.

Alternative Teaching Strategy
Materials: 3 paper circles of the same size, 1 smaller paper circle; 3 paper squares of the same size, 1 larger paper square (see *Teacher Resources*)

Display the circles and ask children to find the circles that are the same size. Then have them describe the circle that doesn't belong: *This circle is smaller*. Repeat the activity with the squares.

Sort by Size
Skill ㉖

Learn the Math

I. Mark an X on the object that does not belong.

2.

3.

Do the Math

Skill ㉖

I. Mark an X on the object that does not belong.

2.

3.

Response to Intervention • Tier 2 **IN111**

IN112 Response to Intervention • Tier 2

© Houghton Mifflin Harcourt Publishing Company

© Houghton Mifflin Harcourt Publishing Company

© Houghton Mifflin Harcourt Publishing Company

Learn the Math

1. Mark an X on the object that does not belong.

2.

3.

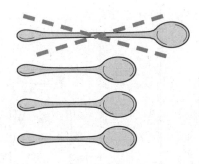

I. Mark an X on the object that does not belong.

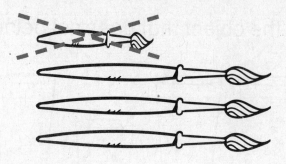

2.

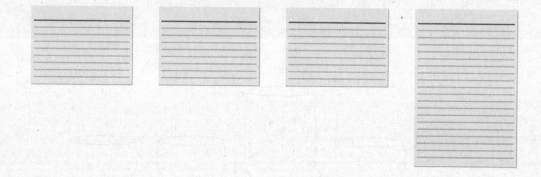

3.

Sort Shapes
Skill 27

Objective
To sort shapes by the number of sides

Materials
Cut-out shapes (see *Teacher Resources*)

COMMON ERROR

- Children may confuse shapes of different sizes and shapes in different orientations.

- Make a group of squares of different sizes. Have children choose a square and count the number of sides. Emphasize that the shapes are different sizes, but they all have 4 sides and 4 vertices. Encourage children to move the squares to show different orientations. Continue with a group of triangles.

Learn the Math page IN115 Have children look at the first exercise as you read the directions. Have them point to shapes as you name them. Help them touch each side as they count the sides aloud. Ask: **Does the shape have three sides? Should we ring it?** Continue with each shape. Use a similar process for Exercise 2 (shapes with 4 sides) and Exercise 3 (shapes with 3 or more sides.)

REASONING Point to a square and a rectangle. Ask: **How are these shapes alike?** Possible answer: they both have four sides.

Do the Math page IN116 Read the directions and talk about Exercise 1. Ask: **Why do we ring the square and the rectangle?** They both have four sides.

Read the directions and help children complete Exercises 2–4. Monitor children as they work.

Children who make more than 1 error in Exercises 1–4 may benefit from the **Alternative Teaching Strategy**.

Alternative Teaching Strategy
Materials: triangle, square, and rectangle shapes (see *Teacher Resources*); two large sheets of drawing paper

Write 3 on one sheet of drawing paper and 4 on the other sheet and explain that it refers to the number of sides in a shape. Have children take turns finding a shape that belongs in one of the groups. After the sorting is completed, help children identify each shape.

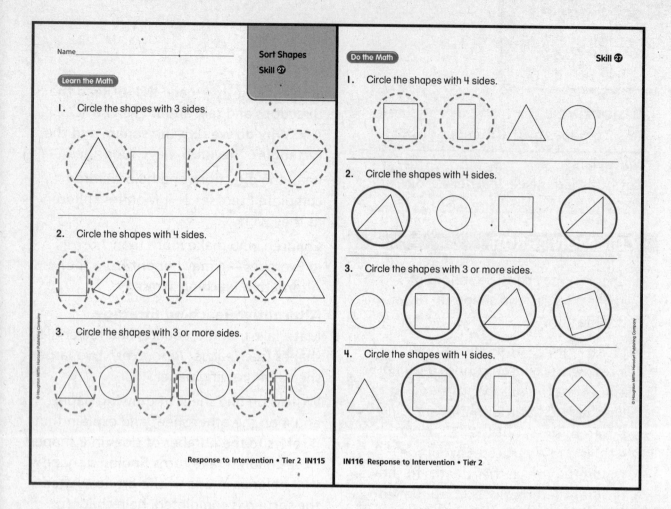

Name_____

Learn the Math

1. Circle the shapes with 3 sides.

2. Circle the shapes with 4 sides.

3. Circle the shapes with 3 or more sides.

Do the Math

1. Circle the shapes with 4 sides.

2. Circle the shapes with 4 sides.

3. Circle the shapes with 3 or more sides.

4. Circle the shapes with 4 sides.

Learn the Math

1. Circle the shapes with 3 sides.

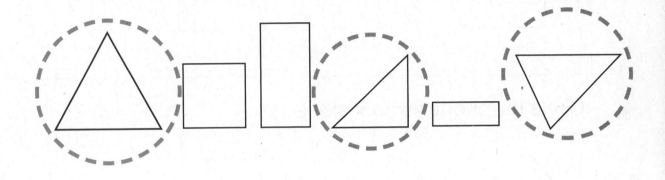

2. Circle the shapes with 4 sides.

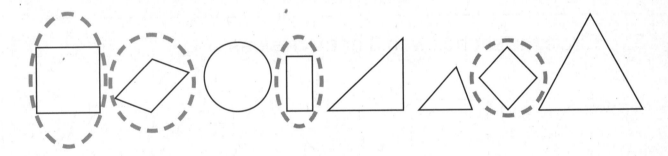

3. Circle the shapes with 3 or more sides.

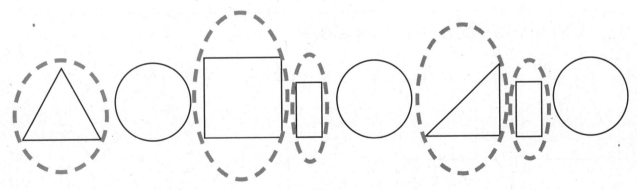

1. Circle the shapes with 4 sides.

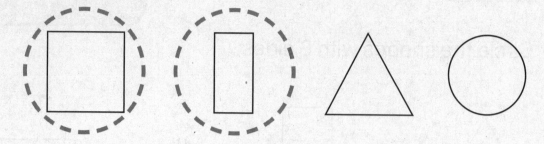

2. Circle the shapes with 4 sides.

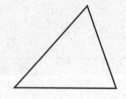

3. Circle the shapes with 3 or more sides.

  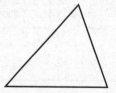 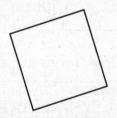

4. Circle the shapes with 4 sides.